The Complete Guide to Self-Discovery & Emotional Healing

Enneagram, Inner Child, and Shadow Work

(3 Books in 1)

Relove Psychology & Sofia Visconti

The Enneagram

A Guide to Determining Your Personality Type, Unlocking the Power of Personal Growth and Self-Discovery

Relove Psychology

TABLE OF CONTENTS

Introduction

The Enneagram can help us break free from our unconscious patterns and live more consciously and authentically. —Sandra Maitri

Have you heard of personality tests like the Myers-Briggs Type Indicator (MBTI) and DISC? They are often used in organizations and personal development for understanding our own behavior and improving our interactions with others. But have you heard of the Enneagram? It's a more comprehensive and fascinating tool that measures our psychological patterns and motivations at cognitive, emotional, and behavioral levels.

We all have different personality traits, and Enneagram helps us understand why we behave and feel the way we do. When we are in a balanced state, we make productive and purposeful decisions. But, when we are stressed or imbalanced, we can become reactive, and our defense mechanisms kick in. The Enneagram helps us identify our potential and shows us how to actualize our best selves.

So, how can we apply the Enneagram in our lives? By becoming more self-aware and practicing self-management, we can make informed decisions and avoid becoming driven by our personality patterns. We can identify our strengths and weaknesses, and work towards our goals by aligning our actions with our higher purpose beyond our ego structure. By doing so, we can overcome challenges and lead a more fulfilling life.

As you read in the quote by Sandra Maitri, the Enneagram can help us break free from our unconscious patterns and live more consciously and authentically, but how? When we have a deeper understanding of ourselves, we can make more conscious choices and live a more fulfilling life.

One way the Enneagram helps us break free from our unconscious patterns is by uncovering our defense mechanisms. These mechanisms are often rooted in childhood experiences and are used to protect ourselves from perceived threats (Booth, 2022). However, these defense mechanisms can become unconscious patterns that limit our ability to grow and develop.

For example, if we have a fear of abandonment, we might develop a pattern of people-pleasing to avoid rejection. This can become an unconscious pattern that limits our ability to assert our own needs and boundaries. By understanding this pattern through the Enneagram, we can work on becoming more self-aware, and break free from this limiting behavior.

While the Enneagram can be a powerful tool for personal growth, there are some common complaints and problems that people may encounter when learning about or using it. One of the most common issues is difficulty identifying their own Enneagram type. The Enneagram is a complex system with nine different types, and it can be challenging to determine which type best describes our personality and motivations.

Another issue is feeling limited by their Enneagram type. While the Enneagram can provide valuable insights into our behavior and patterns, it's important not to box ourselves into one type, or to use it as an excuse for our behavior. We are all complex individuals with unique experiences, and the Enneagram is just one tool among many for self-discovery and growth.

Are you curious about the Enneagram and how it can help you understand yourself—and others—better? If so, this handy guide is packed with valuable insights, practical tips, and powerful tools for exploring the fascinating world of the Enneagram. Whether you're a seasoned Enneagram enthusiast, or you're just getting started, this book has something for everyone. With clear explanations and real-world examples, you'll learn how to identify your Enneagram type, understand your unique strengths and weaknesses, and cultivate greater self-awareness and personal growth.

In this Enneagram book, you'll find a wealth of information on the nine different Enneagram personality types and how they interact with each other. You'll learn how each type approaches life, relationships, and work, and how they respond to stress and challenging situations. You'll also discover how your Enneagram type influences your communication style, decision-making process, and emotional patterns. With practical exercises and insightful advice, you'll be able to apply the

Enneagram to your own life and see tangible results. Whether you're looking to improve your relationships, boost your career, or simply deepen your self-awareness, this Enneagram book is the perfect place to start. So, what are you waiting for? Let's begin!

UNDERSTANDING THE ENNEAGRAM

Chapter 1:
The Nine Enneagram Types

Discovering your personality type can provide valuable insight into your inner workings, including your motivations and how you engage with others. One commonly used theory for determining personality type is the Enneagram system. Identifying your Enneagram type not only piques your curiosity, but also grants you a greater comprehension of the driving forces behind your actions.

However, determining your Enneagram type is only the beginning of the journey. It's equally important to gain a comprehensive understanding of the various types within the Enneagram system. In the following chapter, we will delve into each type and its significance within the Enneagram framework.

According to a study published in the American Journal of Psychiatry, the Enneagram system is characterized as "a personality theory that outlines nine distinct strategies through which the psyche constructs a perspective on the world and interacts with oneself and others" (Alexander & Schnipke, 2020). Psychiatrists have employed this system since the 1970s, and researchers indicate that the theory suggests individuals establish a primary personality strategy to deal with external circumstances by the time they reach adulthood.

The Enneagram system defines nine unique worldviews and motivations, with one of them having the greatest influence on an individual's personality type. These types are not assigned arbitrary numbers; rather, they are categorized into three groups based on the three core aspects of human nature: head types, heart types, and body types. Each group, also known as a triad, is characterized by a central emotion, and driven by a specific center of intelligence (The Nine Enneagram Types [Complete Descriptions], n.d.). While individuals possess traits from all three aspects, the group their personality type belongs to has a greater impact on their life.

To work with the Enneagram, one needs to consciously observe their thoughts, emotions, and behaviors, similar to how mindfulness practices enhance awareness of the present moment. Through this observation of where attention and energy are directed, one can gain valuable insights into their automatic patterns of thinking, feeling, and acting.

The Enneagram can be beneficial in several ways.

First, it can help individuals understand themselves better by shedding light on their motivations, desires, and fears. This self-awareness can lead to personal growth and development, as individuals can begin to identify and work on their areas of weakness and challenge.

Second, the Enneagram can improve interpersonal relationships by increasing empathy and understanding. When individuals understand the motivations and perspectives of those around them, they can communicate more effectively, resolve conflicts more easily, and build stronger relationships.

Third, the Enneagram can be used as a tool for professional development. By understanding their own strengths and weaknesses, individuals can choose careers that align with their values and abilities. They can also identify areas where they need to improve and seek out training or mentorship to develop those skills.

Overall, the Enneagram can provide valuable insights into one's personality, relationships, and career path. By gaining a deeper understanding of oneself and others, individuals can live more fulfilling and meaningful lives.

The Enneagram system outlines nine core types, each with a unique basic fear, basic desire, and typical behavior during times of stress and security. By analyzing these fundamental fears and desires, the Enneagram is able to explain the driving forces behind the behavior. This allows for a comprehensive understanding of each type, which can provide valuable insights into an individual's psychological well-being.

Type One: The Perfectionist

Type One individuals—also known as the "Perfectionists" or "Reformers"—are recognized for their rationality and ethical principles, often working diligently while disregarding their own wants. They harbor a strong desire to be righteous, accurate, and flawless, focusing on values and morality. Furthermore, they are prone to idealize the future, and aspire to improve the world. They may take on the role of a moral compass in their social circles or workplace, guiding others to do the right thing and upholding the values they hold dear. Their dedication to self-improvement and personal growth can be admirable, but it can also become a source of anxiety and stress (Bernes, n.d.).

Type Two: The Helper

Type Twos in the Enneagram—also known as the "Helpers"—possess an inclination to feel helpful and provide assistance to others. They display warmth, affection, and enthusiasm in their approach to supporting others, but in doing so, they can easily disregard their own necessities. These individuals usually exude an amicable and optimistic demeanor; however, they may struggle with overemphasizing the opinions of others. They may struggle with setting boundaries and saying no, as they fear that they will be seen as unhelpful or unlovable if they do not constantly put others first. This can lead to feelings of burnout and resentment if their efforts go unappreciated or unreciprocated (Bernes, n.d.).

Type Three: The Achiever

Type Three, commonly referred to as the "Achievers," are primarily driven by the desire to attain acknowledgment through their accomplishments. Their success is closely tied to their image and public perception. These individuals are goal-driven, competitive, and action-oriented, often pushing themselves excessively to gain the approval of others. They thrive on recognition, praise, and they are highly attuned to the opinions and perceptions of others. This can sometimes lead them to prioritize their public image over their inner feelings and needs. Despite their drive and ambition, Threes may struggle with feeling a sense of inner emptiness or lack of fulfillment. They may struggle to connect with their own emotions, and may use their achievements as a way to compensate for this feeling of inadequacy (Bernes, n.d.).

Type Four: The Individualist

Enneagram Type Four, also referred to as the "Individualists," are recognized for their self-sufficiency and unconstrained nature, which can result in them feeling misunderstood by others. They are recognized as the "seekers" within the Enneagram system, openly contemplating profound inquiries related to their existence, identity, and overall being. Possessing imaginative and analytical traits, these individuals can often experience melancholic tendencies. Fours are often drawn to creative pursuits such as art, music, or writing, as these allow them to express their innermost thoughts and emotions. Their self-sufficiency and individualistic nature can sometimes lead Fours to isolate themselves from others, as they may feel misunderstood, or like they don't fit in. They may also struggle with comparing themselves to others and feeling like they are lacking in some way (Christian, 2021).

Type Five: The Investigator

Type Five, also known as the "Investigators," are inclined towards being curious, analytical, and solitary individuals. They can come across as detached from others, but it's primarily because they treasure privacy and personal space. This type holds a keen interest in discussing topics they are knowledgeable about, emphasizing self-sufficiency and logic as core values. They tend to be logical and objective, using reason and analysis to understand the world around them. At times, Fives may struggle with feelings of inadequacy or fear of not having enough resources, including time, energy, and emotional support. This can lead them to withdraw even further from others, creating a cycle of isolation (Christian, 2021).

Type Six: The Loyalist

Enneagram Type Six, also known as the "Loyalists," demonstrate a high concern for safety and security within the world. Their tendency to anticipate potential mishaps may lead to a perception of being fearful. However, they can exhibit significant courage when it comes to causes that they are passionate about. These individuals are characterized by their sense of loyalty, albeit often coupled with anxiety. They may be prone to self-doubt and second-guessing, constantly seeking reassurance and guidance from others. They may also struggle with decision-making, as they are often highly aware of the potential risks and consequences of each option. Sixes also tend to be highly attuned to social dynamics and the expectations of others. They value structure and hierarchy, often seeking out clear rules and guidelines to follow. They may be prone to conformity and may struggle to assert themselves in situations where they feel uncertain or unsupported (Christian, 2021).

Type Seven: The Enthusiast

Enneagram Type Seven, commonly referred to as the "Enthusiasts," possess a buoyant and vivacious nature, driven by their yearning for joy and delight. These individuals are inclined towards spontaneity, hold a distaste for feeling restricted or confined, and they are always full of energy. They evade emotional distress or discomfort by engaging in activities that bring them pleasure and satisfaction, often keeping themselves occupied. They may struggle with negative emotions, preferring to focus on the positive and avoid anything that might bring them down. This can sometimes lead to a sense of restlessness or dissatisfaction. Despite their carefree and adventurous nature, Sevens may also struggle with commitment and follow-through, due to their desire for new experiences and their tendency to quickly lose interest in ongoing pursuits. They may have a tendency to start new projects or relationships with enthusiasm, only to lose interest or become distracted when things become challenging or less exciting (Booth, 2022).

Type Eight: The Challenger

Enneagram Type Eights are known for their directness, assertiveness, and strength. They tend to have a strong will and desire to be in control, often taking charge of situations and people. This type values independence and self-sufficiency, and they may become confrontational when they feel threatened. They can also display a protective nature towards those they care about, but at times, this may come across as domineering or intimidating (Booth, 2022). Despite their tough exterior, Eights can have a sensitive side, and they desire deep connections with others.

Type Nine: The Peacemaker

Enneagram Type Nines, also known as the "Peacemakers," possess a remarkable ability to consider various perspectives and mediate conflicts. However, they often prioritize others' needs at the expense of their own, sometimes without even realizing it. They tend to go along with the status quo to maintain harmony, even if it means compromising their own desires. Nines may struggle with decision-making, as they tend to see multiple perspectives and fear making the wrong choice. This type values simplicity and stability, preferring a routine and predictable life. They can be easygoing and agreeable, but may struggle with assertiveness and speaking up for themselves (Booth, 2022).

Chapter 2:
The Enneagram's Structure
and How It Works

Over the last decade, the Enneagram, a unique geometric structure with nine points, has gained popularity in the fields of personality testing and career coaching. This system connects the nine points with underlying aspects of the psyche, such as the unconscious mind, to identify fundamental motivations, fears, virtues, fixations, desires, and temptations (How the Enneagram System Works, 2014). If you find this explanation vague, I can help clarify the Enneagram process for you.

The Enneagram unveils the idea that each of the nine personality types holds a unique fundamental belief about the world, which profoundly impacts their motivations, fears, and overall perspective. While these core beliefs are not necessarily incorrect, they can limit our understanding by creating biases and narrow viewpoints. By delving into our Enneagram type and its influence on our perception, we can expand our outlook and approach situations with greater effectiveness. Understanding someone's Enneagram type provides valuable insight into their behavior, as each type possesses distinct core beliefs that consistently drive their actions and decisions. It helps us make sense of behavior that may initially appear puzzling or inconsistent.

In addition, the Enneagram provides insight into how people respond to stress. By detailing how each Enneagram type adjusts and reacts to both stressful and supportive circumstances, the Enneagram highlights avenues for personal growth and establishes a basis for comprehending others.

The Basic Structure

According to Verywell Mind, the Enneagram is represented by a nine-pointed geometric symbol with an outer circle and an irregular hexagon connecting the points, as well as a triangle between points 9, 3, and 6 (Cherry, 2019). The circle represents human wholeness and unity, while the other shapes illustrate how it is divided. The Enneagram includes wings, which are related personality styles that individuals can adopt to develop new facets of themselves. Understanding the influence of wings can add nuance to one's self-understanding. Additionally, each Enneagram type is connected to two other types by lines that represent the person's repressed childhood type and a type they may grow into with further development. These connections illustrate how each type has strengths and challenges, and how personality can change under different circumstances.

In addition to the basic structure of the nine points, wings, and connecting lines, the Enneagram also includes a few other important elements.

For example, each Enneagram type is associated with a deadly sin or passion, which is believed to be at the root of the personality's motivation and behavior (Bayside Church, 2016). These passions are:

1. Type One: anger
2. Type Two: pride
3. Type Three: deceit
4. Type Four: envy
5. Type Five: avarice
6. Type Six: fear
7. Type Seven: gluttony
8. Type Eight: lust
9. Type Nine: sloth

Understanding these passions can help individuals gain greater insight into their own motivations and tendencies.

Another key aspect of the Enneagram is the concept of levels of development. Each Enneagram type has nine levels of development, ranging from healthy and integrated at Level One, to unhealthy and disintegrated at Level Nine. Understanding the levels of development can help individuals recognize their own progress and growth, and identify areas for improvement (How the Enneagram System Works, 2014).

One essential concept in the Enneagram is the idea of integration and disintegration points. These points represent how each type can move towards growth or towards stress, depending on their circumstances. The integration point is the point that a person moves towards when they are healthy and growing. It's the type that they can take on some of the positive qualities of when they're in a good place (Storm, 2020). For example, a Type Five, who tends to be analytical and reserved, might move towards Type Eight , which is more assertive and confident, when they're feeling secure and self-assured.

On the other hand, the disintegration point is the type that a person tends to take on some of the negative qualities of when they're under stress (Storm, 2020). For example, a Type Two, who typically wants to be helpful and supportive, might move towards Type Eight when they're under stress, becoming more aggressive and confrontational. Knowing your integration and disintegration points can be helpful in understanding your patterns of behavior and how to work towards personal growth. By recognizing when you're moving towards one of these points, you can start to make conscious choices to move towards integration and away from disintegration.

The Enneagram also includes a set of subtypes or instinctual variants, which describe how individuals prioritize three key instinctual needs: self-preservation, social connection, and one-on-one relationships. Each Enneagram type can have a different dominant subtype, which can further influence their behavior and motivations (How the Enneagram System Works, 2014).

The Enneagram also includes the concepts of "holy ideas" and "virtues." The holy ideas represent the highest, most enlightened state of each Enneagram type. These ideas are not meant to be religious in nature, but rather spiritual or philosophical. Each type has a unique holy idea that represents its highest potential and serves as a guiding principle for personal growth (Cloete, 2022).

The virtues, on the other hand, represent the positive qualities that each Enneagram type can cultivate in order to move towards their holy idea. Each type has a specific virtue that is associated with their core motivations and fears. By developing this virtue, a person can begin to transcend their core type and move towards a more integrated and balanced state (Cloete, 2022).

Here are the holy ideas and virtues associated with each Enneagram type:

1. The Reformer: Holy Idea—Perfection; Virtue—Serenity

2. The Helper: Holy Idea—Freedom; Virtue—Humility

3. The Achiever: Holy Idea—Hope; Virtue—Truthfulness

4. The Individualist: Holy Idea—Origin; Virtue—Equanimity

5. The Investigator: Holy Idea—Omniscience; Virtue—Non-attachment

6. The Loyalist: Holy Idea—Courage; Virtue—Faith

7. The Enthusiast: Holy Idea—Wisdom; Virtue—Sobriety

8. The Challenger: Holy Idea—Truth; Virtue—Innocence

9. The Peacemaker: Holy Idea—Love; Virtue—Action

It's important to note that the holy ideas and virtues are not meant to be seen as fixed or absolute. Rather, they are aspirational goals that a person can work towards in order to become more integrated and balanced. By cultivating the virtues associated with their Enneagram type, a person can begin to move towards their holy idea and reach their highest potential (Cloete, 2022).

Overall, the Enneagram is a complex and multi-faceted system that offers individuals a comprehensive framework for understanding their personalities, motivations, and opportunities for growth.

How Does it Work?

The consensus among major Enneagram authors is that *everyone is born with a dominant personality type*, which is determined by temperament and other prenatal factors. Each individual emerges from childhood with one of the nine types dominating their personality.

The Enneagram's basic personality type has several noteworthy characteristics.

1. Individuals do not transition from one basic personality type to another throughout their lifetime.

2. The descriptions of the personality types are universal and apply equally to both genders. No type is inherently masculine or feminine.

3. A person's behavior and attitudes may fluctuate between the healthy, average, and unhealthy traits that define their personality type. Not everything in the description will apply to them at all times.

4. Numbers are used to designate each of the nine types, as they are value-neutral and do not imply anything positive or negative. Unlike psychiatric labels, numbers provide a

shorthand way of indicating a lot about a person without being pejorative.

5. The numerical ranking of the types is not significant. A larger number does not equate to a better type, and no type is inherently better or worse than any other.

6. Although some types may be perceived as more desirable in certain cultures or groups, it is important to recognize that each type has unique strengths and weaknesses. The goal should not be to imitate another type's assets, but to become the best version of oneself.

The Enneagram is structured as a 3 x 3 grid that groups nine personality types into three centers based on the predominant way each type processes information. The Centers are the Instinctive, Feeling, and Thinking Centers, each containing three types that share common traits and tendencies of that Center (Enneagram Centers of Intelligence, 2020). For instance, the Feeling Center includes the types that have distinctive strengths and weaknesses in relation to their emotions, such as Type Four. Similarly, Type Eight is in the Instinctive Center, as it has its own set of strengths and weaknesses related to its instincts, and so on for all nine types.

Every person has a unique combination of their basic personality type and one of the two types adjacent to it on the Enneagram's circumference. This combination is known as the person's "*wing*." While the dominant type shapes a person's overall personality, the wing complements it and adds additional, sometimes contradictory, elements to a person's character. Understanding someone's wing is essential to gain a better insight into their personality (How the Enneagram System Works, 2014). For instance, if someone is a type Nine, they will have either a One wing or an Eight wing, and their personality can be best understood by blending the traits of the Nine with either the One or the Eight. However, some people may show little influence from either wing, or may be strongly influenced by their basic type.

The Enneagram traditions differ on whether a person can have one or two wings. Technically, everyone has two wings, as both the types adjacent to their basic type are present in their personality. However, some proponents of the two-wing theory believe that both wings operate equally in everyone's personality. For example, a Type Nine would have an equal amount of both their Eight and One wings.

The Enneagram also recognizes that individuals within each type can be at different *levels of development.*

As I previously explained, the levels of development within each Enneagram type are commonly referred to as the "Levels of Integration" and "Levels of Disintegration," which describe the degree to which an individual has developed the positive or negative traits associated with their type (How the Enneagram System Works, 2014).

The Levels of Integration for each type are:

1. Reformer: Becoming more spontaneous, joyful, and accepting of imperfection.

2. Helper: Developing healthy boundaries and learning to take care of themselves.

3. Achiever: Becoming more compassionate and empathetic towards others, and developing a sense of inner peace.

4. Individualist: Learning to accept themselves as they are and finding a sense of purpose.

5. Investigator: Developing a sense of connection with others and learning to express their emotions.

6. Loyalist: Learning to trust themselves and their instincts.

7. Enthusiast: Developing a deeper sense of meaning and purpose in life.

8. Challenger: Using their strength and power to help others and protect the vulnerable.

9. Peacemaker: Becoming more assertive and learning to express their own needs and desires.

The Levels of Disintegration for each type are:

1. Reformer: Becoming rigid, dogmatic, and losing touch with their own emotions.

2. Helper: Becoming manipulative and resentful towards others and neglecting their own needs.

3. Achiever: Becoming competitive, arrogant, and losing touch with their own values and beliefs.

4. Individualist: Becoming self-absorbed, moody, and losing touch with reality.

5. Investigator: Becoming paranoid, isolated, and losing touch with their own emotions and relationships.

6. Loyalist: Becoming anxious, indecisive, and losing trust in themselves and others.

7. Enthusiast: Becoming scattered, impulsive, and losing touch with their own emotions and relationships.

8. Challenger: Becoming controlling, abusive, and losing touch with their own vulnerabilities and emotions.

9. Peacemaker: Becoming passive-aggressive, stubborn, and avoiding conflict and change.

It is important to note that these levels of development are not fixed or static, and individuals can move up or down the levels throughout their lives, depending on their experiences and personal growth.

While the Enneagram is an incredibly flexible and constantly evolving system, it is important to note that it does not encompass the entirety of human complexity. Each individual has their own unique and often unpredictable traits and behaviors that cannot be fully explained or understood by any single theory or framework. However, the Enneagram can offer valuable insights into certain aspects of an individual's personality and behavior, providing a starting point for deeper understanding and growth.

Chapter 3:
The Enneagram's Origins and Evolution

Despite the unclear origins of the Enneagram, it is evident from all available evidence that it has a rich and intricate history spanning across different cultures and regions. Its roots can be traced back to various mathematical, philosophical, and spiritual traditions (Wagner, 2010).

The Enneagram model as it exists today is a fusion of traditional wisdom and modern psychology. In the following chapter, I will aim to pay tribute to the numerous brilliant minds that contributed to the development of this influential and groundbreaking tool.

A Brief History of the Ancient Roots of Enneagram

The word "Enneagram" is derived from the Greek words "ennéa," meaning "nine," and "gramma," meaning "figure."

Fragments of the Enneagram symbol have been traced back to ancient Greece, where the numerical patterns of three, seven, and nine appeared in epics, myths, philosophy, and mathematical science, emphasizing the significance of this sequence of numbers in ancient works and thought (Wagner, 2010).

Some scholars argue that variations of the Enneagram symbol can be found in the sacred geometry of Pythagorean mathematicians and mystical mathematics (Cloete, 2010).

Pythagoras himself claimed that his theory of numbers, the key to understanding the universe, came from his teacher in Egypt. Respected Enneagram expert Russ Hudson also lectures on the origins of the Enneagram, noting how the Egyptian Enneagram and metaphysical powers and numbers are linked to the origins of the Enneagram .

The founder of Neoplatonism, Plotinus (270 CE), described nine divine qualities that manifest in human nature. His work would later greatly influence Western and Near-Eastern thought through subsequent thinkers such as St. Augustine of Hippo, the Cappadocian Fathers, St. Thomas Aquinas, and Pseudo-Dionysius the Areopagite (Cloete, 2010). The early Greek concepts of vice and virtue were standardized by Christian monks into the seven deadly sins, which became widely recognized.

The first recorded use of a symbol resembling the Enneagram is attributed to Ramon Llull, a Catalan philosopher and theologian. In his work, Ars Magna (1305), Llull posited that there were fundamental truths underlying all fields of knowledge, and that these truths could be understood by studying combinations of elemental principles (Cloete, 2010). He created a diagram consisting of nine sets of aspects in concentric circles, with one of the circles mapping to the Vices of the Enneagram.

Evolution to Its Modern Form

The current understanding of the Enneagram is much clearer than its earlier evolution. George Gurdjieff, a Christian mystic, spiritual teacher, and philosopher of Armenian descent, used the Enneagram and three centers to describe the perpetual motion of creation. Gurdjieff considered movements or sacred dances an essential part of his teachings and referred to himself as a "teacher of dancing." Although he alluded to being introduced to the Enneagram in the 1920s during a visit to an Afghan monastery, he never provided further details on its origin (Cloete, 2010).

The Enneagram gained influence in the 20th century through South American philosopher Oscar Ichazo, who connected the symbol to different personality types through his school, the Arica Institute (The Enneagram Institute, 2014b). Chilean psychiatrist Claudio Naranjo, known for integrating psychotherapy and spiritual traditions, popularized the Enneagram in the professional consulting arena. Naranjo's students, including Ochs, Almaas, and Maitri, spread the Enneagram into Christian communities in the US. Partial validation of the Enneagram has come through experiential and empirical studies since its introduction into psychology. Naranjo's approach to the Enneagram emphasizes the importance of self-awareness and self-transformation. He sees the Enneagram as a tool for understanding the deep-seated psychological and emotional patterns that underlie our behaviors and beliefs.

Naranjo has also written extensively on the Enneagram and its applications in psychotherapy and personal growth. Some of his most influential books include *Character and Neurosis* (1994) and *The Enneagram of Society* (1995).

In the late 1960s, Claudio Naranjo became interested in the Enneagram after meeting Oscar Ichazo and studying with him for a time (Roulo, 2021). Naranjo went on to develop his own understanding of the Enneagram and its application to psychology and psychotherapy. He taught the Enneagram as part of his psychotherapy training programs, and also introduced it to a wider audience through his books and workshops. Naranjo's work with the Enneagram helped to popularize the system in the United States and Europe. He taught the Enneagram at Esalen Institute in California, and later founded the SAT Institute in Chile, which is dedicated to the study of the Enneagram and other spiritual traditions (Roulo, 2021).

Naranjo's approach to the Enneagram emphasizes the importance of self-awareness and self-transformation. He sees the Enneagram as a tool for understanding the deep-seated psychological and emotional patterns that underlie our behaviors and beliefs (Roulo, 2021).

Other influential figures in the development of the Enneagram include Helen Palmer, who popularized the Enneagram in the United States through her books and workshops, and Don Riso and Russ Hudson, who founded the Enneagram Institute and developed their own system of Enneagram typing.

In recent years, the Enneagram has become increasingly popular as a tool for personal growth and development, as well as for understanding and improving relationships. It is used in a variety of settings, including therapy, coaching, leadership development, and spiritual practice.

While the Enneagram has its roots in ancient spiritual traditions and has been adapted and refined over the centuries, its current form as a personality typing system owes much to the work of modern thinkers and practitioners. Despite some controversy and debate over its validity and usefulness, the Enneagram continues to be a popular and widely used tool for self-discovery and personal growth. It has also been integrated into various fields, including business, education, and healthcare.

Some Enneagram enthusiasts have developed their own interpretations and variations of the system, leading to a wide range of Enneagram-related materials and resources available today. This has resulted in some controversy and criticism from those who argue that the Enneagram's original teachings have been distorted and oversimplified.

Despite this, the Enneagram continues to be a popular and widely-used tool for self-discovery and personal growth. Its unique approach to understanding personality types and patterns of behavior has proven useful for many individuals and organizations seeking to improve their relationships, communication, and overall well-being.

THE NINE ENNEAGRAM TYPES

Chapter 4:
Type One–The Perfectionist

Enneagram Type Ones have a strong inclination towards doing things accurately and with high standards. They are known for being meticulous about rules and paying close attention to detail, as well as striving to avoid errors. This often makes them appear to others as perfectionistic, responsible, and demanding individuals (Owens, 2019).

Enneagram Type Ones are often *motivated by a deep desire for perfection* and a belief that the world should adhere to a certain set of standards or principles. They hold themselves to these same high standards, which can lead to self-criticism and a tendency towards being hard on themselves. However, they also have a strong sense of responsibility, and may often take on leadership roles because of their dedication to doing things the "right" way.

Ones can also be *sensitive to criticism or feedback* that challenges their beliefs or methods, as they see it as a personal attack on their integrity. This can lead to rigidity in their thinking and difficulty adapting to change. However, their attention to detail and commitment to doing things correctly can make them valuable assets in many fields, such as law, accounting, or project management.

They are recognized for their *ambitious nature, strong principles, perfectionism, and remarkable self-discipline*. They hold themselves to high standards and constantly aim to enhance their performance, aspiring to reach their full potential.

Key Features in Brief

At the core of Enneagram Type One is a *fear of being flawed, immoral, or corrupt*, while their *ultimate desire is to be virtuous, maintain integrity, and achieve equilibrium*.

Enneagram Type Ones can have a Nine wing or a Two wing. Those with a Nine wing, often referred to as "The Idealist," typically value harmony and inner peace. They seek to create a stable and peaceful environment, often striving to avoid conflict.

Meanwhile, those with a Two wing, known as "The Advocate," have a strong desire to help others and be of service. They believe in being supportive, caring, and generous towards others. They aim to promote positive change in the world, working towards creating a better future for all.

Are You an Enneagram Type One?

If you're uncertain about whether you identify as an Enneagram Type One, there are various online quizzes available. However, if you prefer a quick evaluation, we have one for you. Consider the following 13 statements, which apply to many Type Ones. If at least eight of these statements accurately describe you, it's likely that you're a Type One.

- You're willing to follow instructions, but only if the person giving them is competent.
- You're highly committed to self-improvement and strive to be the best version of yourself.
- You believe that you're usually—or always—right about things.
- You frequently establish goals for yourself and consistently meet them.
- You're willing to sacrifice your own happiness to improve the world around you.
- People have told you that you can come across as critical or condescending.
- You become frustrated when people don't put in enough effort or don't do things correctly.
- You're hard on yourself, even for small errors.
- You seldom lose control of your emotions.
- You've achieved success in your education and/or professional life.
- Merely being happy isn't sufficient; you also need to feel useful.

- You're dependable, and others recognize that they can rely on you.
- Getting affirmation from others is critical to you, even if you don't show it outwardly.

Enneagram Type Ones are often seen as *principled and conscientious individuals who have a strong sense of right and wrong.* They have a natural inclination to live up to their own high standards, which can make them appear rigid or inflexible. However, they are also dedicated and responsible, and are willing to make sacrifices to uphold their values.

Type Ones can be hard on themselves and *may struggle with perfectionism, leading to a tendency towards self-criticism.* They are often high achievers, excelling in their academic or professional pursuits. However, they can also be critical of others when they feel that people are not living up to their own expectations or standards.

Despite their strong sense of duty, Type Ones can also be compassionate and empathetic towards others. They believe that it is their responsibility to make the world a better place and are motivated by a desire to contribute to society. They are also *known for being reliable and dependable*, often taking on leadership roles in their communities or workplaces.

Levels of Development

The Enneagram Type One can experience different levels of development (Type One, n.d.).

Healthy Levels:

1. At their best, Ones become wise and discerning, accepting the world as it is and knowing the best action

to take in each moment. They are compassionate, inspiring, and hopeful, believing that the truth will be heard and that goodness will prevail.

2. Ones at Level Two are conscientious and have a strong sense of personal convictions. They are rational, reasonable, self-disciplined, and moderate in all things. They value morality, personal responsibility, and doing what is right.

3. Ones at Level Three are extremely principled and ethical, always striving to be fair, objective, and just. They have a strong sense of responsibility, personal integrity, and a higher purpose that drives them to become teachers and witnesses to the truth.

Average Levels:

1. At Level Four, Ones become dissatisfied with reality and become high-minded idealists. They believe that it's up to them to improve everything and become advocates and crusaders for causes they believe in. They can be critical of others and explain how things "ought" to be.

2. Ones at Level Five fear making mistakes and strive for consistency with their ideals. They become well-organized, orderly, and often workaholics, while rigidly keeping their feelings and impulses in check. They can be impersonal and puritanical, and their perfectionism can lead to obsession.

3. Ones at Level Six are highly critical of themselves and others, opinionated, and perfectionistic. They often correct people and badger them to do what's right according to their prescriptions. They are impatient,

never satisfied unless things are done according to their standards and can be abrasive, moralizing, and scolding.

Unhealthy Levels:

1. At Level Seven, Ones can become dogmatic, self-righteous, intolerant, and inflexible. They believe they alone know "The Truth," and everyone else is wrong. They can be severe in judgments and rationalize their actions.

2. Ones at Level Eight can become obsessive about the imperfection and wrongdoing of others. They may become hypocritical, doing the opposite of what they preach. They become critical, angry, and punitive, and their perfectionism turns into an obsession.

3. At Level Nine, Ones become condemnatory, cruel, and punitive towards others. They want to rid themselves of wrongdoers, leading to severe depression, nervous breakdowns, and even suicide attempts. They may develop Obsessive-Compulsive and Depressive personality disorders .

Personal Growth Tips For Enneagram Type Ones

Learn to be kind to yourself. Type Ones can have a strong inner critic that can cause them to be hard on themselves, especially during times of stress. However, it is important for Type Ones to be kinder to themselves and to ease up on their inner negative critic. According to Enneagram expert Beatrice Chestnut, Type Ones can benefit from "cultivating an inner voice that is compassionate, encouraging, and supportive." Chestnut suggests that Type Ones can start by imagining how they would speak to a close friend who is going through a difficult time, using the same kind and supportive words with themselves (Chestnut, 2021).

Understand that everyone is following their own journey in life. It is crucial to acknowledge that not everyone is at the same level as you. While Type Ones can be excellent coworkers, mentors, companions, and allies, their strict personal standards may make them appear critical, inflexible, and even difficult to work with to those around them (Brand, 2021). It is essential to develop the ability to appreciate people as they are, and to avoid coming across as preachy or overly concerned with minor details.

Maintain an open perspective. It is important for Type Ones to be open to outside perspectives and understand that people may have different views. While bringing moral clarity and strong principles to work and life is empowering, it is crucial to stay humble and grounded in living those truths, rather than just preaching them. Maintaining an open mind and being receptive to different perspectives can help Type Ones achieve balance in their lives (Brand, 2021).

Manage your self-righteous anger. Your self-righteous anger can be your weakness. You tend to get angry quickly, feeling offended when others do not do things the way you have defined them as right. It is important to step back and understand that your anger can distance people, preventing them from hearing your ideas (Brand, 2021). Moreover, your suppressed anger may lead to health problems like ulcers or high blood pressure, which can lead to more severe health issues in the future.

Embrace your emotions and impulses. To grow and develop, it is crucial for you to acknowledge and embrace your emotions, especially those that stem from your unconscious impulses. You may have a tendency to suppress your feelings and desires, including sexual and aggressive impulses, which are part of being human. Consider keeping a journal or joining a group therapy session to explore and express your emotions in a safe space (Brand, 2021). This can help you realize that you are not alone in your struggles, and others will not judge or condemn you for having human needs and limitations.

Prioritize a healthy work-life balance. While Type Ones' strong work ethic and focus can lead to career success, it's important to prioritize a healthy work-life balance. Type Ones have a tendency to become workaholics, and they may find themselves working late hours at the office, sacrificing time for relationships, family, and self-care. To maintain overall wellness, it's essential to be mindful of the need to balance work and personal life, and to make time for activities outside of work (Brand, 2021). This will not only lead to greater life satisfaction, but it can also prevent burnout and stress-related health issues.

In terms of the specific characteristics of Type One, research has found that individuals who score high on traits associated with conscientiousness—such as organization, self-discipline, and a strong sense of duty—tend to have higher levels of well-being and life satisfaction (Roberts et al., 2014). However, individuals who score very high on conscientiousness can also be prone to anxiety, depression, and perfectionism (Sutin et al., 2010). Overall, while the Enneagram model may not be fully supported by scientific research, there is some evidence to suggest that its types and characteristics may have some validity. Furthermore, the suggested ways of growth for Type Ones align with evidence-based treatments for anxiety, depression, and perfectionism (Type One, n.d.).

Chapter 5:
Type Two–The Helper

According to the Enneagram personality theory, Twos are characterized by their *need for love and a sense of belonging*. They exhibit nurturing, caring and helpful behaviors towards others and are eager to participate in the lives of those around them. They often struggle with saying no when someone asks for their help, as they feel the need to prove their worth by being there for others. Twos fear being alone and unloved, and to cope with this fear, they focus on taking care of others and making themselves central to other people's lives. Their *core motivation is to feel loved and appreciated*, which drives them to express their love towards others through their words and actions (Cain, 2016).

In this chapter, we will explore the core traits, motivations, and fears that define the Type Two personality. We will also discuss common behaviors and tendencies of Twos, including their willingness to assist others, and their struggles with setting boundaries. Through a deeper understanding of this personality type, we can gain insight into our own behavior and that of those around us, ultimately leading to more fulfilling relationships and personal growth.

Key Features in Brief

Enneagram Type Twos are characterized as *empathetic, sincere, and warm-hearted individuals who are inclined to be friendly, generous, and self-sacrificing*. They have a well-intentioned drive to be close to others, but may also engage in people-pleasing behaviors and slip into doing things for others just to feel needed (Schirm, 2022). Their desire to be loved is profound, yet they often struggle with acknowledging their own needs and can become possessive of others.

At their best, Twos are unselfish and altruistic, possessing unconditional love for others. However, their basic fear of being unwanted or unworthy of love can sometimes trigger sentimental or flattering behavior.

Twos with a One wing are known as "Servants," while those with a Three wing are called "The Host/Hostess" (Schirm, 2022).

Key motivations for Type Twos include the desire to be loved, express their feelings for others, be appreciated and needed, and justify their self-image, all of which are intended to elicit a response from others (Don Richard Riso & Hudson, 1999).

Are You an Enneagram Type Two?

To help determine if you might have an Enneagram Type Two personality, take this five-question quiz and answer with a "yes" or "no" to each question:

- Do you enjoy forming close relationships with others?
- Would people describe you as caring?
- Do you find it difficult to say "no" when someone asks you for help?
- Do you engage in acts of service or give back to your community—such as volunteering or donating money—?
- Would you say you are non-judgmental?

If you answered "yes" to most of these questions, there's a good chance you have a Type Two personality. However, keep in mind that the Enneagram is a complex personality system, and taking a deeper dive into all nine types can help provide a more comprehensive understanding of your personality and personal growth opportunities.

Levels of Development

The levels of development for this type are as follows:

Healthy Levels:

1. When someone reaches this level, they become truly selfless, humble, and caring. They possess an altruistic nature, showing unconditional love to both themselves and others. They consider it a privilege to be a part of other people's lives (Type Two, n.d.).

2. At this level, individuals are empathetic and compassionate. They genuinely care about others' needs and show thoughtfulness and warmth. They are forgiving, sincere, and deeply concerned about the well-being of those around them.

3. People at this level are encouraging and appreciative. They have the ability to see the good in others and believe in the importance of service (Type Two, n.d.). While they prioritize taking care of others, they also understand the need to nurture and give to themselves. They embody true love and generosity.

Average Levels:

1. Those at this level yearn for closer connections with others. They tend to engage in people-pleasing behaviors, becoming excessively friendly and emotionally expressive. They have good intentions but may seek approval, flattery, and attention. Love is a central value for them, and they often talk about it (Type Two, n.d.).

2. People at this level become overly intimate and intrusive. They have a strong need to be needed, resulting in their tendency to hover, meddle, and try to control others under the guise of love. They expect something in return for their efforts, leading to mixed messages (Type Two, n.d.). They can become possessive and codependent, going to great lengths to fulfill the needs of others while neglecting their own.

3. At this level, individuals start to feel self-important and self-satisfied. They believe they are indispensable, although they may overestimate their impact on others. They might develop hypochondria and adopt a "martyr"

mindset, sacrificing themselves for the sake of others. They can become overbearing, patronizing, and presumptuous.

Unhealthy Levels:

1. People at this level can be manipulative and self-serving. They use guilt to make others feel indebted to them and often inflict suffering on others. They may turn to food and medication to suppress their emotions and gain sympathy (Type Two, n.d.). They undermine others through belittling and disparaging remarks. They deceive themselves about their motives and display aggressive or selfish behavior.

2. Those at this level become domineering and coercive. They feel entitled to get whatever they want from others, including repayment of old debts, money, or even sexual favors.

3. At this level, individuals excuse and rationalize their actions. They feel abused and victimized by others, which fuels their bitterness, resentment, and anger. They somatize their aggression, resulting in chronic health issues. They "fall apart" and burden others as a way to seek validation. This level is often associated with Histrionic Personality Disorder and Factitious Disorder (Type Two, n.d.).

Personal Growth Tips For Enneagram Type Twos

Practice mindfulness. Enneagram Type Twos can benefit greatly from practicing mindfulness, which involves stepping outside of themselves and observing their personality objectively. By taking a step back, they can observe patterns in their thoughts, feelings, and behaviors, allowing them to gain a deeper understanding of their own needs and desires (Type Two, n.d.). This process can help Twos set healthy boundaries and prioritize self-care, which in turn can lead to personal growth and development. By becoming more self-aware, Twos can break free from their need to be needed by others, and find fulfillment and purpose within themselves.

Embrace self-awareness. Enneagram Type Twos tend to prioritize the emotions and needs of others, often neglecting their own. In order to grow, it's important for Twos to acknowledge and accept their own emotions (Type Two, n.d.). By taking note of their own feelings about things, Twos can better understand their own needs and desires. This process can be aided by activities like journaling, which can help Twos get more in touch with their emotions. By embracing self-awareness and prioritizing their own emotions, Twos can develop a greater sense of self-acceptance, and find more balance in their relationships with others.

Learn to ask and accept "no." As an Enneagram Type Two, you have a natural gift for intuiting the feelings and needs of others. However, it's important to remember that what you think others need may not always align with their actual desires. To cultivate healthy relationships and personal growth, it's crucial to ask others what they need before jumping in to offer assistance (Type Two, n.d.). Effective communication involves clearly communicating your intentions, and being open to the possibility of receiving a "no" in response. It's important for Type Twos to understand that a rejection of their particular offer of help does not equate to a rejection of them as a person. Learning to ask and accept "no" can help Twos develop a more balanced and respectful approach to helping others, while also practicing self-care and boundary-setting.

Practice humility in your good deeds. Instead of seeking recognition and appreciation for your good deeds, practice humility. It's important to remember that helping others should come from a genuine desire to do so, not for the sake of gaining recognition or validation. Avoid drawing attention to your good deeds or reminding others of your past acts of kindness. Instead, focus on helping others without any expectation of recognition or reward. This will not only improve your relationships, but also allow you to experience the joy of helping others for its own sake.

It is important for Type Twos to remember that their desire to help others should come from a place of genuine love and care, rather than a need for validation or a fear of being alone. By learning to set healthy boundaries and practice self-care, Type Twos can continue to express their love and generosity towards others while also taking care of themselves.

Chapter 6:
Type Three–The Achiever

Threes are individuals who are driven to *achieve and stand out from others, as they desire to feel important and valuable.* They may come across as confident, ambitious, and focused on their goals to those around them. However, despite their outward appearance, Threes often struggle with feelings of self-doubt and a lack of intrinsic self-worth, seeking validation through their accomplishments (Enneagram Type 3: The Achiever, 2021). They tend to prioritize their image and how others perceive them, wanting to be seen as successful.

The *biggest fear for Threes is the possibility of being seen as insignificant or failing,* so they strive to excel in all aspects of life as a way to prove their worth (Enneagram Type 3: The Achiever, 2021). Their core motivation stems from a deep-seated need for attention and admiration, which drives them to be successful and significant in order to avoid feeling worthless.

Key Features in Brief

Individuals who identify with the Enneagram Three personality type tend to be *confident, attractive, and charismatic* (Enneagram Type 3: The Achiever, 2021). They possess strong ambition, competence, and energy, and are often driven to advance their status. While diplomatic and poised, they can become overly preoccupied with their image and what others think of them. They may also struggle with workaholism and competitiveness.

At their best, Threes are authentic, self-accepting role models who inspire others.

Threes can become consumed by their pursuit of success and validation, often at the expense of their well-being and relationships (Enneagram Type 3: The Achiever, 2021). Their sense of self-worth is tied to external achievements and recognition, and they may engage in deceitful and manipulative behavior to maintain their image.

Threes have a strong sense of their own identity and are self-accepting. They are able to recognize their strengths and weaknesses without judgment, and can pursue their goals without losing sight of their values and relationships. They are often successful, but they no longer define their worth solely by their achievements.

Threes are *motivated by a fear of worthlessness and a desire to feel valuable and worthwhile.* Depending on their wing type, Threes may be known as "The Charmer"—when they have a Two wing—or "The Professional" when they have a Four wing. Their key motivations include seeking affirmation, attention, admiration, and the desire to distinguish themselves from others by impressing them (Enneagram Type 3: The Achiever, 2021).

Are You an Enneagram Type Three?

If you are curious about whether you might be an Enneagram Type Three, I have created a short quiz consisting of five yes or no questions to help you assess your fit with this personality type. Read the questions below and answer them based on your intuition:

- Do you enjoy being the center of attention?
- Do you typically excel in whatever you do?
- Is it important for you to be perceived as successful?
- Do others often look to you for guidance or leadership?
- Would your friends and family describe you as popular or well-liked?

If you answered "yes" to at least three of these questions, it is possible that you may be a Type Three.

Levels of Development

The levels of development for this type are as follows:

Healthy Levels:

1. At this level, Threes are self-accepting, authentic, and humble. They have a fullness of heart and are benevolent towards others.

2. Threes are self-assured, confident, and charming. They have a high level of self-esteem and adaptability (James, 2021).

3. Threes are ambitious, but not for personal gain. They strive to be outstanding in order to embody widely admired cultural qualities.

Average Levels:

1. At this level, Threes become highly concerned with their performance and achieving their goals. They compare themselves with others and strive for exclusivity and being the "best."

2. Threes become overly concerned with their image and how they are perceived by others. They may lose touch with their own feelings and have problems with intimacy (James, 2021).

3. Threes become narcissistic, exhibiting grandiose notions about themselves and their talents. They become arrogant and contemptuous of others.

Unhealthy Levels:

1. At this level, Threes become exploitative and opportunistic, willing to do whatever it takes to preserve the illusion of their superiority (James, 2021).

2. Threes become devious and deceptive in order to hide their mistakes and wrongdoings. They become malicious and may betray or sabotage others to triumph over them (James, 2021).

3. At the most unhealthy level, Threes become vindictive and seek to destroy others' happiness. They become obsessed with destroying anything that reminds them of

their own shortcomings and failures, exhibiting psychopathic behavior (James, 2021).

Personal Growth Tips For Enneagram Type Threes

Practice truthfulness. To truly develop and grow, Enneagram Type Three individuals must prioritize honesty, both in their relationships with themselves and others. It is crucial to acknowledge and express genuine feelings and needs, rather than suppressing or hiding them in favor of projecting an image of success or importance. The temptation to impress others with exaggerated accomplishments must be resisted, as true authenticity and vulnerability are what truly leave a lasting impression on others.

Learn to slow down. To truly thrive, it's vital for a Type Three to learn how to slow down. When constantly striving for success and recognition, it's easy for them to overlook the present moment or take it for granted. That's why it's crucial for them to pause, relax, and appreciate the here and now. This includes turning off their smartphones and disconnecting from the frenetic pace of life, even if only for a little while. By taking a break from their never-ending to-do list, Threes can recharge and reconnect with themselves, which will ultimately help them achieve their goals with more focus and clarity.

Develop deeper connections through active listening. To cultivate deeper connections with others, it is important for Threes to practice active listening. Often, Threes are so preoccupied with how they are perceived by others that they miss out on opportunities to form meaningful relationships (Cherry, 2019). Active listening involves being fully present in the conversation and giving the speaker your undivided attention. This means putting aside distractions, such as smartphones, and avoiding the urge to steer the conversation back to yourself. By truly hearing what others have to say, Threes can gain a better understanding of those around them and build stronger connections.

Overcome the fear of vulnerability. Threes may find it daunting to embrace vulnerability as it involves revealing their true selves to others, not just the image they want to project. However, personal growth and development require them to confront this fear and become more authentic. By learning to embrace vulnerability, Threes can break down emotional barriers and forge deeper connections with others, ultimately leading to greater personal fulfillment.

Type Three individuals must balance their ambition for success and efficiency with empathy and honesty. They can experience personal growth by releasing the notion that their worth depends on how others perceive them. At times, they may need to take the risk of losing others' approval to follow their genuine desires and live with authenticity. A healthy Three prioritizes sincerity over accomplishments, and understands that their value is not solely based on what they produce or achieve.

Chapter 7:
Type Four—The Individualist

According to Ryan Lui, a certified Enneagram practitioner, Fours are commonly referred to as the "individualist" who have a *strong desire for an ideal world*. Their perspective is that of the glass being half-empty, and they yearn for it to be full, with a deep longing for a sense of completeness in life (Regan, 2021).

Enneagram educator Julie Nguyen explains that Fours are *inherently independent and free-spirited individuals*. Their identity is often intertwined with their emotions, leading them to follow what feels right in the moment, which can sometimes result in unfinished projects (Regan, 2021).

Fours desire a *sense of uniqueness, beauty, and completeness in their lives, but they also fear being alone, average, or that their current life is all there is.* They have weaknesses such as being self-centered, envious, and dramatic, but they are also self-aware, passionate, and introspective.

Key Features in Brief

According to Ryan Lui, Fours highly *value individuality, authenticity, and originality, and they also embody these qualities themselves.* They enjoy feeling unique, and want everything in their life to hold meaning and beauty (Regan, 2021).

Lui explains that *Fours are emotional individuals*, which can influence their work and relationships. They have a tendency to get carried away in their daydreams and feelings, which can lead to intense emotions that may sometimes overwhelm others. Enneagram educator Julie Nguyen further states that Fours seek heightened emotional states, which can make them lose touch with reality. Julie Nguyen also states that Fours are romantics who are highly aware of the potential for good in the world. However, this type of mindset can also give birth to negative thinking or depression if they focus too much on what could be, rather than being grateful for what they already have (Regan, 2021).

Fours are *known for their creativity and sensitivity*, which makes them highly reflective and artistically inclined. They have strong self-awareness and can express themselves well. However, this self-awareness can also cause self-centeredness. (Regan, 2021).

Are You an Enneagram Type Four?

Although there are many detailed resources available for exploring your Enneagram type, I can help you get started with a quick five-question quiz just like you did in the previous chapters to determine if you may be a Type Four. By answering these questions with a simple "yes" or "no," you can find out if you fit into this type.

- Do you often feel like your emotions are more intense than those of the people around you?
- Do you enjoy spending time alone to explore your dreams, thoughts, talents, and artistic interests?
- Do you sometimes find yourself indulging in sadness or melancholy?
- Do you ever feel like nobody truly understands you or that your identity is too complex for others to connect with?
- Do you have a tendency to compare yourself to others, sometimes feeling like you fall short?

If you answered "yes" to most of these questions, it's possible that you could be an Enneagram Type Four!

Levels of Development

Just like the previous Enneagram types, Type Fours have their own levels of development that we will explore in this section.

Healthy Levels:

1. Type Fours are deeply creative individuals who express both personal and universal concepts through their work, often creating something that is self-creative, inspired, and regenerative.

2. Type Fours are highly self-aware and introspective, often on a quest for self-discovery, and they are sensitive to their own feelings and those of others. They are gentle, compassionate, and tactful.

3. Type Fours are true to themselves and highly individualistic. They are emotionally honest, self-revealing, and humane (Enneagram Type 4 – the Individualist, 2021). They have an ironic view of self and life, can be both serious and funny, and are emotionally strong and vulnerable at the same time.

Average Levels:

1. Level 4 of the Type Four Enneagram is characterized by an artistic and romantic orientation to life. Individuals at this level seek to create a beautiful and aesthetic environment to cultivate and prolong their personal feelings. They are often highly attuned to beauty and seek to express themselves through art or other creative outlets. They may also have a strong need for authenticity and self-expression, and may resist conforming to societal norms or expectations. While there are many positive aspects to this level, there can also be some negative consequences (Enneagram Type 4 – the Individualist, 2021). They can become self-absorbed, introverted, and overly sensitive, leading to moodiness, shyness, and self-consciousness.

2. Fours tend to internalize everything and take everything personally. They tend to focus on their inner experiences and can become self-indulgent and self-absorbed, which can make it hard for them to connect with others. If Type Fours at this level don't learn to manage their emotions and get out of their heads, they may become stuck in their

patterns of withdrawal and self-absorption, leading to further isolation and unhappiness (Enneagram Type 4 – the Individualist, 2021).

3. Type Fours gradually start to believe that they are different from others and become increasingly disdainful, decadent, sensual, and prone to living in a fantasy world (Enneagram Type 4 – the Individualist, 2021). They may experience self-pity and envy of others, leading to self-indulgence and impracticality.

Unhealthy Levels:

1. This level represents an unhealthy state where a person experiences a deep sense of shame and self-loathing. They become self-inhibiting, angry at themselves, and depressed. They feel alienated from themselves. People at this level may become very critical of themselves, seeing only their flaws and failures. They may also become judgmental of others and feel that they are not understood or appreciated.

2. At this level, individuals may feel tormented by delusional self-contempt, self-hatred, self-reproaches, and morbid thoughts. They may become increasingly isolated and disconnected from others, feeling that they are fundamentally flawed and unworthy of love and acceptance (Enneagram Type 4 – the Individualist, 2021). They may see everything as a source of torment and blame others, driving away anyone who tries to help them.

3. The unhealthy tendencies of Type Four reach their peak. They experience a deep sense of despair and hopelessness, feeling like they have lost all sense of purpose or direction in life. They may become self-

destructive, engaging in reckless behaviors such as substance abuse or self-harm, in an attempt to escape their emotional pain. At this level, individuals with Type Four may also experience thoughts of suicide or engage in suicidal behaviors (Enneagram Type 4 – the Individualist, 2021).

Personal Growth Tips For Enneagram Type Fours

Practice gratitude. In addition to helping with feelings of inadequacy, practicing gratitude can also improve overall well-being and mental health. Research has shown that gratitude practices can increase positive emotions, reduce stress, and improve sleep (Emmons & McCullough, 2003). For Enneagram Type Fours, who may be prone to negative emotions and a focus on what's missing or lacking in their lives, a regular gratitude practice can help shift their perspective towards the positive aspects of their lives and promote greater overall satisfaction.

Separate self from feelings. It is crucial for Enneagram Type Four individuals to understand that their feelings do not define them. They should avoid equating themselves with their emotions as they are not a true source of support. According to "Personality Types" by Don Richard Riso and Russ Hudson, "one of the most important mistakes Fours make is to equate themselves with their feelings." (Don Richard Riso & Hudson, 1999) It's common for Enneagram Type Fours to become deeply attached to their emotions, using them as a primary source of self-understanding. However, this can often lead to a distorted view of the self, and an overemphasis on negative emotions. Therefore, it's essential for Fours to recognize that their feelings are not the ultimate source of support or guidance. Instead, they should strive to understand themselves holistically, considering their thoughts, actions, and experiences in addition to their emotions.

Prioritize consistent productive work. Don't delay taking action until you feel like you are in the "right mood". Enneagram Type Four individuals may have a tendency to wait for inspiration to strike, or to put off tasks until they feel motivated. However, the reality is that they are happiest and most fulfilled when they are working on something productive that aligns with their values and interests (Regan, 2021). Waiting for the perfect mood or inspiration can lead to procrastination and a lack of progress towards their goals.

Embrace constructive feedback to grow. It is crucial for individuals with a type Four Enneagram personality to be receptive to constructive feedback, both positive and negative. It's important to recognize that negative feedback is not an attack on their identity, and positive feedback should not be disregarded or dismissed. Feedback, whether it's criticism or praise, can provide valuable insights and lessons to help them grow and develop. By embracing feedback, Fours can gain a better understanding of themselves and their interactions with others, leading to more fulfilling relationships and a deeper sense of personal growth.

Fours possess a keen sense of appreciation for beauty, intricacy, and uniqueness, and value depth and meaning over superficiality. They are capable of confronting the darker aspects of life without the need to gloss over them. Envy is a major weakness for Fours, as they often compare themselves unfavorably to others who possess qualities they believe they lack (Regan, 2021). It's important for them to remember that every individual has what they need to be themselves, and there's no Enneagram type that's better or worse than others. The strengths and weaknesses of each type manifest differently in every person, depending on their level of maturity. While Fours could benefit from being more selfless and less self-pitying, they are fundamentally independent, creative, and authentic individuals who are in tune with their emotions and desires.

Chapter 8:
Type Five–The Investigator

According to the Enneagram personality system, Fives possess a *cerebral, analytical, and independent nature*. They are driven by a desire to comprehend the world around them, and safeguard their autonomy and privacy to live life on their own terms. Fives tend to examine and dissect information extensively to achieve a thorough understanding before taking any action. While they excel at thinking logically, Fives may *struggle to step outside of their own thoughts and engage with others*. Their inclination to withdraw and keep to themselves can make it challenging for others to understand their inner workings. Fives possess an insatiable curiosity and love to acquire knowledge, which they stockpile like squirrels hoarding nuts for the winter. They prefer to use reason and knowledge as the basis for their decisions, rather than being overwhelmed by emotions. Fives *tend to detach from their feelings and analyze them objectively* (Type Five, n.d.).

Key Features in Brief

Enneagram Five is commonly referred to as The Investigator, owing to their *keen desire to comprehend the underlying mechanisms behind various phenomena*. Fives are highly curious individuals who seek to understand the workings of the world around them, whether it pertains to the natural world, the cosmos, or the inner workings of their own mind. They are *known to approach everything with a critical eye*, frequently challenging accepted beliefs and conducting their own research to test the validity of assumptions. Fives are relentless in their pursuit of knowledge, always seeking to delve deeper and discover new insights.

Fives derive significant benefits from their *ability to concentrate on tasks without being derailed by their emotions*. They are often able to maintain a sense of composure and level-headedness in situations where others may become agitated. However, this strength can also have a downside. Due to their natural inclination towards privacy, Fives may struggle to share personal information with others, preferring to keep their thoughts and feelings to themselves. They may feel that revealing too much about themselves could make them vulnerable to others' demands or expectations. As a result, they may be better at acquiring information than forming intimate connections with others.

When Fives have a Type Four wing, their *emotional expression is enhanced*, allowing them to better communicate and understand their feelings, rather than solely analyzing them. They may become more interested in exploring their creative side and experimenting with new ideas.

On the other hand, when Fives have a Type Six wing, their *observational skills are combined with the foresight of the Six.* They may become more social and better able to contribute to group efforts. Their thinking may shift towards practical problem-solving, and they may develop a stronger, family-oriented social instinct that values stability.

Are You an Enneagram Type Five?

Let's try out the quiz once more. Simply answer with a "yes" or "no" response without overthinking.

- Do you enjoy exploring new concepts, even if they are unfamiliar to you?
- When confronted with a problem, is your initial response to analyze and research it thoroughly before taking action?
- Do you tend to keep your thoughts and emotions private, only sharing with those you trust deeply?
- Do you often misplace objects because you are preoccupied with your thoughts?
- Do you have a tendency to intellectualize your feelings, analyzing them rather than fully experiencing them?

If you have answered at least three or more questions in the affirmative, there's a high chance that you are an Enneagram Type Five.

Levels of Development

Type Five individuals can experience various levels of development, with distinct behaviors and attitudes associated with each level.

Healthy Levels:

1. Type Fives become visionaries, seeing the world from a broad and profound perspective while remaining open-minded. They make groundbreaking discoveries, and innovate new ways of perceiving and doing things (Robledo, 2022).

2. Fives are highly intelligent, curious, and perceptive individuals who possess an unquenchable thirst for knowledge. They are able to concentrate deeply on their interests, anticipate what's coming next, and see patterns and connections where others might miss them. This level of perceptiveness and intelligence makes them valuable in many fields, particularly in science, research, and academia (Robledo, 2022).

3. Enneagram Type Fives reach a high level of competence and expertise in their chosen field of interest. They are driven by their passion for knowledge, and they are excited by the prospect of acquiring new information. They may become pioneers in their field, developing innovative and creative ideas that can be extremely valuable and original. They possess a highly individualistic and idiosyncratic nature, which often leads them to pursue unconventional paths.

Average Levels:

1. Individuals become increasingly focused on conceptualizing and fine-tuning everything before taking

action. They prefer to work things out in their minds, often engaging in model building, preparing, practicing, and gathering more resources. Their approach is studious, and they are continually acquiring new techniques to apply to their interests (Robledo, 2022). At this level, Enneagram Type Fives also become more specialized, and their pursuit of knowledge can sometimes make them seem "intellectual." They often challenge accepted ways of doing things, and seek to discover new and innovative approaches.

2. As they become more detached and preoccupied with their thoughts, Level 5 Fives may retreat from the practical world and become absorbed in offbeat, esoteric subjects.

3. At Level 6 of development, these individuals become increasingly antagonistic towards anything that they perceive as a threat to their inner world and personal vision. They become more provocative and abrasive in their interactions with others, intentionally taking extreme and radical views. This behavior stems from their fear of losing control and feeling overwhelmed by their environment (Robledo, 2022). Type Five individuals at this level may become very cynical and argumentative, engaging in intellectual debates and discussions solely for the sake of proving themselves right and others wrong.

Unhealthy Levels:

1. At this level of development, Enneagram Type Fives become reclusive and isolated from reality. They become eccentric and nihilistic, rejecting and repulsing any social attachments or relationships. They see the world as a

harsh and unforgiving place, and they are convinced that they are too weak to survive in it (Type Five, n.d.).

2. At this level, they become overwhelmed and consumed by their fears and threatening ideas, leading to horrifying delusions and phobias. They begin to see threats everywhere and are often paranoid and suspicious of others' intentions. They may experience panic attacks, nightmares, and other forms of severe anxiety as they struggle to cope with their overwhelming fears (Type Five, n.d.).

3. At this level, the individual seeks oblivion and may resort to self-destructive behavior or even commit suicide. This level of development generally corresponds to the most severe forms of mental illness, including schizophrenia (Type Five, n.d.).

Personal Growth Tips For Enneagram Type Fives

Embrace the idea of seeking help when needed. Enneagram Type Fives have a tendency to desire complete independence and self-sufficiency (Robledo, 2022). However, it's important to recognize that there are people in your life who would be more than willing to lend a hand if you asked. Whenever you find yourself overwhelmed or overloaded, take a moment to consider if there's anyone who can help you with your tasks. Don't be hesitant to seek support when necessary.

Engage in physical activities to promote relaxation. To combat the tendency to overthink and dwell in their thoughts, Enneagram Type Fives can benefit from engaging in physical activities that promote relaxation and mindfulness. Hobbies like running, dancing, yoga, and other activities that involve movement can help Fives get out of their heads and into their bodies, allowing them to unwind and enjoy the present moment. By prioritizing these activities, they can develop a healthy outlet for stress and anxiety, improving their overall well-being.

Embrace the unknown. Instead of fixating on finding all the answers, it can be helpful for Enneagram Type Fives to accept the unknown and embrace ambiguity. It's important to realize that not having all the information or answers doesn't mean failure or inadequacy. Instead, consider taking action based on what you do know, and trust your ability to problem-solve as situations arise. Practicing mindfulness and meditation can also help to reduce the need for constant mental stimulation, and give space to simply be in the present moment.

Recognize distractions and prioritize tasks. Be mindful of when you are investing a lot of time and energy in projects or hobbies that don't align with your goals or improve your self-esteem. While it's okay to explore different interests, they can become distractions from what you really need to do. Taking decisive action towards your priorities can bring more confidence than simply acquiring more knowledge or skills.

Share your knowledge and skills. Instead of hoarding your knowledge and skills like a dragon, sitting on a pile of treasure, share them with others. The world needs what you have to offer, and giving to others will only increase your options in the long run. Holding onto things may make you feel secure, but it can ultimately lead to deprivation. Remember that generosity is key to building lasting connections and increasing opportunities.

Enneagram Type Five individuals often struggle with trusting others, being emotionally vulnerable, and making themselves available in different ways. Unfortunately, their fear of relationship problems can often lead to self-fulfilling prophecies (Robledo, 2022). However, it's crucial to recognize that conflicts in relationships are natural, and it's healthier to work through them than to withdraw into isolation. Remember, building connections with others takes time and effort, but the rewards are worth it.

Chapter 9:
Type Six—The Loyalist

Sixes prioritize stability, striving to mitigate risks and align themselves with dependable authorities and institutions. They *remain watchful and attentive, anticipating potential hazards and taking preemptive measures to avoid them.* Their biggest fear is being caught off guard and incapable of protecting themselves from harm. To manage this fear, they try to prepare for any conceivable circumstance (Type Six: The Loyalist, n.d.).

Sixes *exhibit a steadfast, devoted and dependable nature,* preferring to maintain enduring relationships and ideas that provide a sense of security in an unpredictable world. They are considerate and meticulous, proficient at anticipating and guarding against potential difficulties (Type Six: The Loyalist, n.d.). They approach problem-solving systematically, and are adept at playing the role of a critical evaluator.

Although Sixes *excel at operationalizing and executing projects,* they may become entrenched in a pattern of anticipating worst-case scenarios and fixating on future uncertainties.

Key Features in Brief

Type Sixes are known as Loyalists. This moniker *derives from their reputation for being the most trustworthy, devoted, and faithful personality type.* They are known for their reliability, resolute nature, amiability, and a sharp sense of humor (Type Six: The Loyalist, n.d.). These individuals can be thought of as guardians and cautious skeptics, always anticipating and prepared for what's ahead. They are passionate about the greater good, and are capable of seeing what others may overlook.

Sixes are *highly skilled and proficient individuals* who invest a significant amount of effort in developing their abilities. They work diligently, and are meticulous in their approach. Despite their concerns about potential mishaps, they are *remarkably brave and capable in emergencies.* On the other hand, Sixes have difficulty initially trusting others and tend to overthink, worrying about potential problems that could arise at any moment (Type Six: The Loyalist, n.d.).

During their formative years, Sixes *internalize the notion that the world is perilous and that their authority figures cannot provide them with safety.* Consequently, they develop an acute sensitivity to minor signals that may indicate danger, and safeguard themselves by attempting to anticipate every potential threat and hazard.

Type Sixes with a Five wing exhibit attributes akin to those of Type Fives, displaying a *tendency toward independence and introversion*. They are less inclined to place their trust in others, and prefer to maintain their own counsel.

In contrast, Type Sixes with a Seven wing individuals possess qualities resembling those of Type Sevens, such as being *outgoing and sociable*. They excel at meeting people's needs, and often relish being part of organizations or groups.

Are You an Enneagram Type Six?

Would you like to determine whether you possess the traits of an Enneagram Six personality type? If so, continue reading. In this chapter too, I have crafted a five-question quiz to assist you in making this determination. Simply respond with a "yes" or "no" to the following inquiries:

- Do you frequently advocate for the people in your life?
- Do you have a tendency to worry or feel anxious about potential risks or dangers?
- Do you seek feedback from loved ones before making decisions?
- Do you often question authority figures and challenge the status quo?
- When making decisions, do you take into consideration how your actions may affect others?

If you responded "yes" to the majority of the aforementioned questions, it is highly probable that you possess the traits of a Six.

Levels of Development

Enneagram Type Six can be divided into nine levels of development, ranging from healthy to unhealthy.

Healthy Levels:

1. Enneagram Six individuals are at their healthiest and most developed state. They are confident, self-assured, and able to navigate life's challenges with ease. They are able to balance their independence with their need for connection with others. They are able to form symbiotic, interdependent relationships that are based on mutual trust and support. They are reliable and responsible, and are able to create stability and security in their world (Francis & Singletary, 2022).

2. They have a positive and optimistic outlook, and they are able to inspire and motivate others with their confidence and enthusiasm. They are natural leaders, and their belief in themselves and their abilities leads to true courage, positive thinking, leadership, and rich self-expression. They are able to balance their need for security with their desire for independence, and they are able to maintain healthy relationships based on trust, respect, and mutual support (Francis & Singletary, 2022).

3. They often take on leadership roles and become excellent team players. They are confident in their abilities, and possess a strong sense of purpose. They become community builders, responsible and reliable, and build trust with those around them. They are hardworking, persevering, and often sacrifice their own interests for the greater good (Francis & Singletary, 2022).

Average Levels:

1. Sixes start investing their time and energy into whatever they believe will be safe and stable. However, at this level, their constant search for security can lead to anxiety, and a lack of trust in themselves and others. They may become overly attached to rules, procedures, and structures, and fear change and uncertainty. This can cause them to resist new ideas and challenges, becoming inflexible in their thinking (Francis & Singletary, 2022).

2. Sixes may develop a defensive attitude towards others to avoid being burdened with more responsibilities or demands. This can lead to passive-aggressive behavior, where they become evasive, indecisive, and hesitant in their interactions. They may also become cautious, procrastinate, and show ambivalence towards situations, leading to contradictory and mixed signals. The internal confusion they experience can make them react unpredictably, appearing highly reactive, anxious, and negative towards others (Francis & Singletary, 2022).

3. Sixes tend to compensate for their insecurities by adopting a confrontational and defensive attitude towards others. They become sarcastic and belligerent, blaming others for their problems and taking a tough stance towards those they perceive as "outsiders". Despite their tough exterior, they are actually fearful of authority, and highly suspicious of others. This can lead them to become paranoid and conspiratorial, as they try to silence their own fears. Overall, at this level, Enneagram Six types are trapped in a cycle of fear and defensiveness, which can make it difficult for them to form healthy relationships and achieve their goals (Francis & Singletary, 2022).

Unhealthy Levels:

1. Sixes become highly divisive, disparaging, and berate others who do not share their beliefs. They start to feel like they are in a constant state of crisis, and may become overly reactive to even minor challenges or setbacks.

2. At this level, Sixes' behavior becomes increasingly extreme and fanatical, leading to outbursts of anger and aggression. They may become obsessed with conspiracy theories and alternate realities that reinforce their beliefs of being targeted and under attack (The Enneagram Institute, 2014a).

3. Sixes experience extreme anxiety and a sense of impending doom. They feel like they have ruined their security, and are now defenseless against whatever they perceive as a threat. In extreme cases, Enneagram 6 types at level 9 may exhibit self-destructive and suicidal behavior. They may turn to alcoholism, drug overdoses, or engage in other self-abasing behaviors (The Enneagram Institute, 2014a).

Personal Growth Tips For Enneagram Type Sixes

Overcome self-fulfilling prophecies. When you obsess over a fear or a worry, it can become a self-fulfilling prophecy, leading to unintended consequences. This is especially true for people with the Enneagram type Six personality, who tend to allow their fear to lead to extreme paranoia (Personality Type: Six – the Loyalist or Skeptic, n.d.). To avoid this, it's important for Sixes to recognize when they are over-fixating on their fears and to take steps to calm their anxieties before they spiral out of control.

Challenge catastrophic thinking. Enneagram Type Six personalities are known for their tendency to overthink and imagine worst-case scenarios, leading to anxiety and fear (Personality Type: Six – the Loyalist or Skeptic, n.d.). However, this habit of overthinking can be broken by challenging catastrophic thinking and embracing the present moment. Keeping a journal can be an effective tool in this process as it allows you to reflect on your worries and track how often they materialize in reality.

Recognize pessimism. Enneagram Type Six individuals may struggle with managing their emotions, particularly when upset or angry, and may even turn on others and assign blame for their own mistakes or misfortunes. Additionally, their tendency towards pessimism can lead to dark moods and negative thought patterns that may project onto reality, causing further distress. To overcome these patterns, it's important to recognize the effects of pessimism, and the potential for self-sabotage. One way to break this cycle is to actively challenge negative thought patterns and reframe pessimistic views. This can be done through practices such as cognitive-behavioral therapy or mindfulness techniques.

As Type Six individuals confront their anxieties and recognize that the world is not as perilous as they once believed, they can achieve a state of health and inner peace. This newfound sense of self-esteem enables them to trust their own judgments and opinions, as well as stand up for themselves without submitting blindly to authority or feeling the urge to rebel against it. As a result, they can quietly and confidently make meaningful contributions to their community, demonstrating both serenity and courage.

Chapter 10:
Type Seven–The Enthusiast

Sevens are *driven by their thirst for adventure and their aversion to boredom and pain.* They are known for their vibrant and exuberant demeanor, always eager to try new things and explore the world around them.

Their love for excitement and their desire to live life to the fullest make them appear *lively and fun-loving* to others. They have a reputation for being hedonistic, seeking pleasure and avoiding anything that might cause them discomfort.

Sevens are constantly on the move, hopping from one activity to another in their quest to experience everything life has to offer. Their *busy and active lifestyle* is fueled by their fear of missing out on the good things in life and getting stuck in a monotonous routine (Enneagram Type 7, 2022).

Key Features in Brief

Sevens are *brimming with enthusiasm for life*, eagerly embracing new experiences and opportunities. Their inquisitive nature and positive outlook make them the eternal optimists, always seeing the bright side of any situation. This personality type is appropriately named "The Enthusiast" because Sevens approach life with an *unwavering sense of curiosity and adventure*. They are like children in a candy store, excitedly anticipating all the wonderful things life has to offer (Sarikas, 2020).

Sevens are known for their bold and vivacious personalities, tackling challenges with a cheerful determination. *They possess a unique quality, often described as "chutzpah," a combination of brashness and nerve.* Driven by their fear of missing out and their desire to experience everything life has to offer, Sevens embrace their sense of adventure and embark on new journeys with infectious enthusiasm (Enneagram Type 7, 2022).

Type Sevens with a Six wing exhibits some Six-like traits that set them apart from other Sevens. They tend to be *more skeptical, self-disciplined, and practical, often taking a cautious approach to new experiences (Sarikas, 2020).* In times of crisis, they can be reliable and responsible leaders, valuing loyalty and productivity. This type may find fulfillment in careers that allow them to combine their love for adventure with their desire for structure and responsibility. Examples of such professions include pilot, tour guide, detective, travel agent, and journalist.

On the other hand, Type Sevens with an Eight wing , share qualities with the Type Eight, making them *more assertive, confident, and career-focused than other Sevens* (Sarikas, 2020). They have a fearless attitude and encourage others to pursue their goals with vigor. They may find success in careers that allow them to utilize their natural charisma and leadership abilities, such as law enforcement, motivational speaking, television news, management, and sales.

Are You an Enneagram Type Seven?

If you are confused about your personality type and trying to figure out whether you are an Enneagram Type Seven, then here is a quick quiz for you:

- Do you often find yourself daydreaming about new adventures and experiences?
- Do you tend to avoid situations that could potentially cause discomfort or pain?
- Do you get restless or anxious when you're stuck in the same routine for too long?
- Do you enjoy being the life of the party and making people laugh?
- Do you have a hard time committing to long-term plans or projects because you fear missing out on other opportunities?

If you responded "yes" to the majority of the aforementioned questions, it is highly probable that you possess the traits of a Seven.

Levels of Development

Now, let's discuss the different levels of development for the Type Seven Enneagram personalities.

Healthy Levels:

1. When Type Seven Enneagram individuals are at their best, they have the ability to thoroughly absorb their experiences and cultivate a profound sense of gratitude and appreciation for what they have. They become amazed by the simple pleasures of life and are filled with joy and ecstasy. This heightened state of being also allows them to have glimpses of spiritual reality and recognize the unlimited goodness of life (Mukherjee, 2021).

2. One of the defining characteristics of Type Seven individuals is their ability to find joy and pleasure in even the most mundane aspects of life. They possess an insatiable curiosity and are constantly seeking out new and exciting experiences. They thrive on adventure, variety, and spontaneity and are often drawn to activities that offer a rush of adrenaline or excitement. This makes them very lively and vivacious, as they are quick to express their enthusiasm for anything that captures their attention.

3. Individuals are known for their ability to easily achieve success in a variety of areas. They possess a multitude of talents and are often considered to be generalists who can do many different things well. This makes them highly versatile and adaptable, able to excel in a wide range of environments.

Average Levels:

1. Individuals become increasingly restless and desire more options and choices in their lives. They have a strong need for adventure and new experiences, which often leads them to become "worldly wise" and knowledgeable about a wide range of topics. However, this desire for new experiences can also make them less focused and more easily distracted. Their desire for constant stimulation and novelty can also lead to a sense of emptiness from within or dissatisfaction (Mukherjee, 2021).

2. Type Sevens become increasingly hyperactive and struggle to discriminate what they truly need. They have difficulty saying "no" to themselves, and often throw themselves into a constant state of activity in order to stave off boredom. However, this can lead to a lack of focus and follow-through, as they become involved in too many things at once.

3. Individuals may be addicted to various forms of excess, whether that be material possessions, food, or other indulgences. They may become hardened and insensitive, with a sense of jadedness that prevents them from fully appreciating the pleasures of life (The Enneagram Institute, n.d.-b).

Unhealthy Levels

1. Their desire to escape from their anxieties may lead to impulsive and reckless behavior, as they struggle to control their impulses and may act out in ways that are harmful to themselves and others. They may struggle to know when to stop and may fall into the trap of addiction and excess (Mukherjee, 2021).

2. At this level, individuals may be in flight from themselves, avoiding dealing with anxiety and frustration. They may act out their impulses rather than confronting their issues. They may engage in compulsive behaviors, such as manias or other excessive activities, in an attempt to distract themselves from their internal struggles.

3. Type Seven individuals at Level Nine of the Enneagram are characterized by deep despair and a tendency towards self-destruction. They may feel panic-stricken and claustrophobic, struggling to cope with their internal struggles (The Enneagram Institute, n.d.-b).

Personal Growth Tips For Enneagram Type Sevens

Overcome impulsivity. By resisting the urge to act on every impulse, you can focus your energy on what is truly beneficial for you. This can help you avoid engaging in behaviors that may be harmful or counterproductive in the long run.

Learn to embrace pain. Rather than always seeking out distraction and avoiding discomfort, it can be helpful to pause and check in with yourself when you feel the need to escape from difficult emotions. By acknowledging and accepting painful experiences, you can begin to see the beauty and growth that can come from navigating through challenging times.

Cultivate meaningful connections. While it can be tempting to keep things light and avoid uncomfortable conversations, doing so can prevent you from forming deeper and more meaningful connections with others. By being willing to go below the surface and share your authentic self, you can build trust, intimacy, and understanding with those around you.

Practice delayed gratification. It's easy for Sevens to get caught up in the excitement of the moment and want to have everything immediately. However, it's important to remember that not everything needs to be acquired right away. Take a step back, and assess whether the acquisition is truly necessary or just a temporary desire. By delaying gratification, you may find that you are better able to make decisions that align with your long-term goals and values.

Prioritize quality over quantity in your experiences. Sevens have a tendency to seek out as many new and exciting experiences as possible, but it's important to remember that the quality of an experience is more important than the quantity (Enneagram Type 7 - the Adventurer, n.d.). Focus on being fully present in the moment and giving your full attention to the experience at hand, rather than constantly anticipating the next one. By doing so, you may find that you are able to fully appreciate and enjoy the present experience, leading to greater satisfaction in the long run.

Chapter 11:
Type Eight—The Challenger

Eights are characterized by their *strong desire to wield power and control,* while avoiding any hint of vulnerability (Alderson, 2022). They project an assertive, confident, and resolute image to those around them. They may come across as intimidating and argumentative at times, but this behavior stems from their need to stand up for their beliefs and defend the vulnerable.

Individuals who identify as Eights *possess remarkable levels of intensity, energy, and determination*. They exude an aura of power and toughness, and they relish the opportunity to demonstrate their strength in the face of adversity. Eights are known for their willingness to engage in open confrontations and their reluctance to back down from a challenge. Eights have been given the moniker of "The Challenger" due to their propensity for embracing challenges themselves and presenting others with opportunities to push themselves beyond their limits.

Eights are the *epitome of "rugged individualists" within the Enneagram framework*. They value their independence above all else and strive to remain self-sufficient, resisting the notion of being beholden to anyone. Eights often reject societal norms and conventions, and they have the ability to overcome their shame, fears, and concerns about consequences (Alderson, 2022). While they may take into account others' opinions of them, Eights remain steadfast in their own convictions and actions. They approach their endeavors with an unwavering determination that can inspire awe, and sometimes even intimidation in those around them.

Key Features in Brief

Challengers are *driven by their goals and take pride in their self-competence.* They blaze their own trail fearlessly and take great satisfaction in their independence and sharp intellect. Even when they stumble, Challengers hold their heads high and pick themselves back up, emerging stronger than before (Doyle, 2022b).

Eights are *fierce advocates for others*, particularly those who are marginalized, oppressed, or vulnerable. They have a strong sense of justice, and *view the world through a lens of "strong" and "weak" individuals.* They identify themselves as strong, and view it as their responsibility to safeguard those who are not. During childhood, Eights may have been *labeled as "bossy" by their peers.* Many Eights come from environments with high levels of conflict and feel the need to develop a robust personality at an early age to cope and survive (Mukherjee, 2023).

Eights with a Seven wing are *more outgoing and exude vitality* thanks to the influence of the playful, extroverted, and life-affirming Type Seven. These Eights find it easier to enjoy life's pleasures, and they are inclined to channel their energy into initiatives that leave behind a positive impact (Mukherjee, 2023).

Eights with a Nine wing become more approachable and measured. They are *less combative and more open to mediating and negotiating.* These Eights often bring a calm, grounded presence to their confidence, are more oriented towards family and warmth, leading by protecting, rather than intimidating others (Mukherjee, 2023).

Are You an Enneagram Type Eight?

Here are five yes or no questions to determine if someone might have an Enneagram Type Eight personality:

- Do you enjoy being in control and taking charge of situations?
- Are you comfortable with confrontation and open conflict?
- Do you have a strong desire to protect and defend the weak and vulnerable?
- Are you hesitant to show vulnerability or admit weakness?
- Do you consider yourself an independent thinker who doesn't follow social conventions easily?

If you responded "yes" to the majority of the aforementioned questions, it is highly probable that you possess the traits of an Eight.

Levels of Development

Let's briefly discuss the nine levels of development of the Type Eight individuals.

Healthy Levels:

1. At their best, Enneagram Type Eight personalities become self-controlled and generous. They learn to be compassionate, patient, and tolerant by surrendering themselves to a higher authority. They exhibit bravery, even risking their lives to achieve their goals, with a desire to leave a lasting impact on the world. In this state, they may attain true heroism and may even be remembered throughout history for their greatness (Doyle, 2022b).

2. At this level, individuals become self-assured, assertive, and strong. They develop the ability to advocate for their needs and desires confidently. Their "can-do" attitude and strong inner drive make them resourceful and determined. They are able to face challenges head-on and have a firm belief in their ability to overcome any obstacles (Doyle, 2022b).

3. Eights become even more confident and assertive. They have a natural ability to take charge and make things happen, becoming decisive and authoritative leaders that others look up to. Eights in this level champion those around them, acting as providers and protectors who carry others with their strength. They are honorable and

take pride in their ability to use their power and influence for the greater good (Doyle, 2022b).

Average Levels:

1. They may become focused on accumulating wealth, power, and prestige, using their assertiveness and dominance to climb the ladder of success. They place great importance on self-sufficiency and financial independence. At this level, they may deny their own emotional needs and focus solely on acquiring resources and asserting their power (Type Eight: The Challenger, n.d.).

2. At this level, Type Eights become preoccupied with maintaining control and power, and may become confrontational and intimidating to protect their position. Fearful of being vulnerable and losing influence, they may resort to using force or manipulation. They start acting like the "boss" whose word is law (Type Eight: The Challenger, n.d.).

3. At this level, they may become vindictive, seeking revenge on those who have crossed them or threatened their power. These individuals may become paranoid and see enemies everywhere. They also struggle to find inner peace and satisfaction, despite their external success and accomplishments (The Enneagram Institute, n.d.-a).

Unhealthy Levels:

1. At this level, individuals with Enneagram Type Eight may reach a state where they fiercely resist any form of control and become absolutely ruthless, adopting a "might makes right" mentality. This could lead to a

criminal or outlaw-like behavior, where they turn into renegades or con-artists.

2. At this level, Type Eights develop grandiose beliefs about their power, invincibility, and capacity to overcome any obstacle. This leads to megalomania, where they feel all-powerful and invulnerable. They take on too much, often recklessly over-extending themselves beyond their capabilities (Type Eight: The Asserter, n.d.).

3. This level represents the extreme and most unhealthy manifestation of Type Eight. At this level, individuals with this personality type may develop delusions of grandeur and a false sense of invincibility, leading them to recklessly overextend themselves. They may become violent, vengeful, and destructive, exhibiting sociopathic tendencies and a complete disregard for the well-being of others. If they perceive themselves to be in danger, they may resort to brutal and murderous behavior rather than surrendering to anyone else. This level generally corresponds to the Antisocial Personality Disorder (The Enneagram Institute, n.d.-a).

Personal Growth Tips For Enneagram Type Eights

Practice mindful decision-making. As a type that relies on their body and instinct, Eights tend to act impulsively on their emotions, leading to hasty decisions and outbursts. It's important for them to pause and reflect on their thoughts and emotions before taking any action. By practicing mindful decision making, Eights can gain better control over their reactions, and avoid impulsive behavior. Taking time to sort through their thoughts and feelings before reacting can lead to more thoughtful and effective decision-making.

Embrace vulnerability as a strength. It's important to understand that vulnerability is not synonymous with weakness. If you find yourself equating the two, take a moment to explore why that is. Connect with your inner child and recognize that vulnerability takes great courage. Instead of fearing it, embrace it as a strength. This can be challenging, but it's a worthwhile pursuit. Through vulnerability, you can experience deeper levels of intimacy and connection with others.

Learn to yield. As an Eight, it can be challenging to yield to others, even in small situations where little is at stake. However, it's crucial to recognize that constantly desiring to dominate others is a sign of an inflating ego, which can lead to more significant conflicts in the future. Therefore, it's essential to learn to yield occasionally, and allow others to have their way without sacrificing your power or needs.

Challenge your negative beliefs. Despite what you might believe in moments of stress, the world is not always against you. While it can be challenging for Eights to let their guard down and accept support from others, it is essential for their growth and well-being. Challenge your negative beliefs, and recognize that there are people in your life who care about you and want to support you.

Balance your intensity with self-care and respect for others' boundaries. As an Eight, you have a passionate zest for life that can lead to overindulgence and boundary-crossing (Enneagram Type 8 Description, n.d.). It's important to find a balance by practicing self-care and respecting others' boundaries. Don't hesitate to seek the help of a friend or partner to remind you when you're going too far. Remember that moderation can be a life saver, and neglecting your health can have serious consequences. Prioritize your well-being and that of those around you.

Chapter 12:
Type Nine–The Peacemaker

Nines are known for their *peaceful and harmonious nature*, which makes them pleasant companions (The Enneagram Type 9: The Peacemaker, 2022). They prefer to avoid conflicts and emotional turmoil and strive to maintain a serene inner state. However, they can sometimes be firm in their opinions. Despite their tendency to adjust to their environment, they have an aversion to being instructed and might respond in a non-confrontational manner when they sense pressure.

One of the *biggest fears of Nines is being overly dependent on others and potentially alienating them*. To avoid this, they tend to go along with what others want, striving to be accepted and valued by those around them.

The personality type Nine is referred to as The Peacemaker because they are *deeply committed to achieving inner and outer peace*, not just for themselves, but also for those around them (The Enneagram Type 9: The Peacemaker, 2022). Nines are often spiritual seekers with a strong desire to connect with both the universe and others.

Key Features in Brief

Peacemakers *possess a gentle and amiable nature*, making them skilled at mediating and counseling within a group of friends or colleagues. They put in a lot of effort behind the scenes to ensure that the group's harmony remains steady and undisturbed. Since childhood, Peacemakers have been adept at getting along with their classmates, and they make valuable contributions to group projects. They have a knack for viewing a situation from multiple perspectives, and refrain from hastily drawing conclusions (Wagner, 1980).

Nines are *unassuming and modest individuals* who prioritize maintaining stability. They appreciate and value the small things in life and take pleasure in the simple joys. Nines are widely admired by almost everyone for their inclusive and considerate nature, providing a safe environment for people to express themselves freely. However, they *tend to suppress their own opinions and desires*, often saying yes to others before considering their own needs. They tend to avoid conflict, even when it may be beneficial for their personal growth (Wagner, 1980).

When a Nine has an Eight wing , they receive several characteristics of the assertive nature associated with the type Eight personality. Nines with an Eight wing tend to be *more*

energetic, self-assured, and pragmatic. They also have a greater ability to tap into their anger and are more willing to confront conflicts.

When a Nine has a One wing, the Type One personality influences them to *become more disciplined, organized, and self-assured.* Having a strong One wing can greatly assist Nines in discovering their own unique voice, as they tend to hold themselves to a higher standard of morality and may be more inclined to express their viewpoints to others.

Are You an Enneagram Type Nine?

Here's a yes or no personality quiz for Type Nine:

- Do you value inner peace and harmony in your relationships and surroundings?
- Do you sometimes struggle to express your own opinions and desires in order to keep the peace with others?
- Do you have a tendency to procrastinate or delay making decisions?
- Do you feel a strong connection to spirituality or a higher power?
- Are you usually easy-going and agreeable in group settings?

If you responded "yes" to the majority of the aforementioned questions, it is highly probable that you possess the traits of a Nine.

Levels of Development

Let's explore the nine levels of development of the Type Nine Enneagram:

Healthy Levels:

1. Type Nines become self-assured and experience a deep sense of fulfillment, achieving a state of contentment and equanimity because they are present and fully engaged with themselves. They possess a paradoxical quality of being at one with themselves, which allows them to form more profound relationships with others. They feel intensely alive and are fully connected to themselves and those around them (Hook et al., 2020).

2. Nines have a heightened appreciation for the beauty of everyday life and take pleasure in the simple things. They are patient, unpretentious, and good-natured, embodying a genuine kindness that stems from their desire to create a harmonious environment. They are not motivated by material wealth or social status, but rather by the desire to live a peaceful and fulfilling life (Hook et al., 2020).

3. Nines possess a keen ability to see the bigger picture and understand the perspectives of others. They are adept at finding common ground and creating a peaceful resolution to conflicts. They have a talent for synthesizing different opinions and ideas, creating a unified vision that everyone can agree on.

Average Levels:

1. Nines tend to fall into conventional roles and expectations, not asserting their own individuality and creativity. They become passive, allowing others to make decisions for them, and go along with the status quo without questioning it. They may use philosophies and stock sayings to deflect others and avoid confronting their own issues.

2. Nines become more disengaged from reality and become increasingly complacent. They tend to become mentally hazy and start indulging in comforting fantasies to distract themselves from reality. They become indifferent to the world around them, unwilling to exert themselves or make any significant effort (Hook et al., 2020).

3. Type Nine individuals become increasingly focused on maintaining peace and avoiding conflict, even at the cost of their own needs and desires. They may become stubborn and fatalistic, feeling as though they have no control over their circumstances or the people around them. They may avoid taking action to address problems, preferring to minimize them or to simply hope that they will go away on their own.

Unhealthy levels:

1. Type Nines may neglect their responsibilities and become a danger to themselves and others. They may feel powerless, helpless, and trapped in their own world, unable to see a way out. Others may become frustrated and angry by their lack of action and disconnection from reality.

2. Type Nines experience pathological dissociation, in which they attempt to block out anything that could potentially affect them, leading to a complete loss of connection with reality (The Enneagram Institute, 2021). They become depersonalized, numb, and lose the ability to function in their daily lives. In this state, Nines may feel as if they are in a dreamlike state or watching themselves from afar. They may struggle to remember things or have difficulty focusing, making it hard to carry out even basic tasks.

3. The Type Nine individual has completely abandoned themselves and their desires, becoming a shattered shell of a person. They may have extreme difficulty making decisions or taking any action, and may rely heavily on others to make decisions for them. They may also experience hallucinations or delusions, and have a distorted sense of reality (The Enneagram Institute, 2021).

Personal Growth Tips For Enneagram Type Nines

Acknowledge your own desires. Nines tend to prioritize the needs and desires of others, often neglecting their own (Doyle, 2022c). They may feel that their own wants and needs are not as important as those of others, and they fear that asserting themselves will lead to conflict. However, this habit of neglecting themselves can limit their potential for personal growth and fulfillment. To break this habit, Nines need to pay attention to their own wants and needs. This means taking the time to reflect on their thoughts and feelings without any external influence. They can start by asking themselves questions like, "what do I want?" and "what do I need?". They can also try journaling or meditating to connect with their inner selves and gain a deeper understanding of their own desires.

Shift your perspective on conflict. Instead of immediately avoiding any kind of conflict, try to reframe your thinking about it. What might seem like a major disagreement to you might actually be a minor issue to the other person. Before disengaging from the situation, take a moment to remind yourself that the stakes are often lower than you initially perceive them to be.

Build assertiveness. If you find it challenging to be direct and assertive in conversations, start practicing with the people you feel most comfortable with. Gradually, work your way up to communicating more assertively in everyday situations. This will help you build the confidence to speak up for yourself when you need to. Remember, being assertive is not the same as being aggressive. Assertiveness involves expressing your thoughts and feelings in a clear and respectful manner, while still being open to listening to others. It allows you to set healthy boundaries and take control of your life. So, don't be afraid to start small, working your way up to more challenging situations. The more you practice being assertive, the more natural and effortless it will become.

Embrace discomfort as a path to growth. Instead of avoiding challenging situations, try staying with them and seeing them through to the other side. Remember that growth often comes from discomfort, and that facing difficult situations can help you become a stronger and more resilient person. Focus on the positive outcomes that can come from staying with something difficult, rather than on the discomfort in the moment. With practice, you can learn to embrace discomfort as a path to growth and transformation.

When you encounter a decision that feels overwhelming, resist the urge to seek advice from others right away. Instead, take some time to reflect on your own thoughts and feelings. What do you truly want in this situation? What are your personal values and priorities? Trust yourself to make the decision that aligns with your own desires and needs. Remember, it's okay to make mistakes and learn from them. Taking ownership of your decisions can lead to a stronger sense of self-confidence and self-reliance.

ENNEAGRAM AND PERSONAL DEVELOPMENT

Chapter 13:
Using the Enneagram for Self-Discovery

The idea of self-discovery may conjure up images of meditating while burning incense, but in reality, it's a practical, ongoing journey that ebbs and flows with the ups and downs of life. There are times, like this past month, when I naturally feel more introspective and reflective. While I need daily moments of quiet reflection, these more intense periods prompt a deeper search for self and my place in relation to the divine.

The diversity of human experience fascinates me. We can be in the same moment, yet perceive it differently based on our unique perspectives and temperaments. My life experiences have heightened my awareness of the importance of understanding my own lens, and that of those I care for. It's a beautiful journey, though I acknowledge that uncovering the truth about myself can be bitter at times, as it brings to light my hidden fears, shame, and anger. However, this is where I've found the deepest healing and self-compassion.

Our personal outlook on life shapes our preferences and actions, from our taste in food to how we spend our leisure time. Though our individual perspectives define us, they can also limit our ability to appreciate alternative viewpoints, hindering our personal growth and development.

Why is Self-Discovery Important?

Self-discovery can have several benefits, including enhancing one's self-awareness and intuition, as well as increasing self-worth and the ability to stand up for oneself (Carroll & Ivanoff, 2016). Additionally, self-discovery can help individuals identify and name their emotions, understand their sources, and reframe negative self-talk into positive self-talk. This process can also help people set boundaries in relationships by understanding their values and what they are willing to tolerate. Moreover, self-discovery can help individuals identify their fears and work towards overcoming them, as well as diagnose and work on bad habits while building better ones. Finally, self-discovery can help people set more meaningful goals by gaining a better understanding of their desires and aspirations (McLeod, 2022).

Let's Start the Inner Work

The Enneagram is a powerful tool for self-discovery that can help individuals understand their unconscious patterns and motivations. However, the Enneagram is not just a personality typing system; it is also a tool for inner work and personal growth. The Enneagram can assist individuals in identifying their fears, desires, and automatic responses, which can be challenging but can also lead to personal transformation.

The inner work with the Enneagram involves becoming aware of one's habitual patterns, emotional triggers, and automatic responses. By recognizing these patterns, individuals can begin to understand the root causes of their behaviors, and how they relate to their Enneagram type. This self-awareness can lead to a greater sense of empathy and compassion towards oneself and others.

Furthermore, the Enneagram offers a unique approach to personal growth by emphasizing the integration of all nine types. Individuals can learn from the strengths and weaknesses of each type and incorporate them into their personal development. For example, an individual who identifies as a Type Five can learn from the Type Two by exploring the importance of relationships and connection in their lives.

The Enneagram also highlights the importance of practices such as mindfulness, self-compassion, and self-reflection in personal growth. These practices can help individuals become more present and aware of their thoughts, emotions, and behaviors, and can also aid in breaking free from limiting beliefs and patterns.

In conclusion, the Enneagram can be a powerful tool for individuals looking to embark on a journey of self-discovery and personal growth. The inner work with the Enneagram involves becoming aware of one's habitual patterns, emotional triggers, and automatic responses, and utilizing this knowledge to develop greater self-awareness, empathy, and compassion. By integrating the strengths and weaknesses of all nine types and engaging in mindfulness, self-compassion, and self-reflection practices, individuals can unlock their full potential and transform their lives.

Potential Challenges and Pitfalls of Using Enneagram for Self-Discovery

While the Enneagram can be a powerful tool for self-discovery and personal growth, there are also potential challenges and pitfalls that individuals may encounter when using this system.

One of the main challenges is the risk of mistyping. Identifying one's Enneagram type can be a complex and nuanced process that involves self-reflection, self-awareness, and sometimes the guidance of a trained professional. However, there is a risk of individuals mistyping themselves or others, which can lead to inaccurate information and hinder personal growth (Belle, 2020).

Another potential challenge is the risk of becoming overly identified with one's Enneagram type (The Enneagram Model Explained and Why It Isn't Always a Good Idea, n.d.). While understanding one's Enneagram type can provide valuable insights into one's patterns and behaviors, it is important to remember that the Enneagram is not meant to define individuals as static or limited beings. Instead, it is a tool for self-awareness and personal growth, and individuals should strive to cultivate a sense of openness and flexibility in their approach.

Additionally, the Enneagram can be a deeply personal and emotional journey, and it may bring up difficult or uncomfortable feelings for individuals. It is important to approach this process with self-compassion, and a willingness to explore and work through these feelings.

Another pitfall of using the Enneagram for self-discovery is the temptation to use it to justify or reinforce negative patterns or behaviors (The Enneagram Model Explained and Why It Isn't Always a Good Idea, n.d.). For example, an individual who identifies as a Type Eight may use their Enneagram type to justify aggressive or confrontational behavior, rather than using it as a tool for understanding and transforming those patterns.

Finally, it is important to remember that the Enneagram is just one tool for self-discovery and personal growth. It is not a substitute for professional therapy or other forms of support, and individuals should seek out additional resources as needed (Belle, 2020).

All in all, while the Enneagram can be a valuable tool for self-discovery and personal growth, it is important to approach it with mindfulness, self-awareness, and a willingness to work through potential challenges and pitfalls. By staying open to the process and seeking out additional support as needed, individuals can use the Enneagram to unlock their full potential and transform their lives.

Chapter 14:
Understanding Your
Strengths and Weaknesses

The Enneagram is not just about identifying your type, but also about understanding the interconnectedness of all the types. Each type has a unique perspective and gifts to offer, and by recognizing and appreciating these differences, you can build stronger and more diverse relationships. It isn't just about putting a label on your personality; it's about discovering your unique strengths and weaknesses. It requires being honest with yourself about areas where you struggle, as well as areas where you shine. Remember, it's totally okay not to be perfect all the time, or to fit perfectly into one Enneagram type. Your instincts may lead you in that direction, but the more you learn about yourself, the more control you can exercise over your choices. So, don't worry if you don't always excel—that's all part of the journey!

How Does the Enneagram Help You Understand Your Strengths and Weaknesses?

Have you ever wondered what drives your behavior and thought patterns, or what areas you need to work on to improve yourself? The Enneagram is a powerful tool that can help you gain self-awareness and understand your strengths and weaknesses. But, you have already learned this in the previous chapters.

By identifying your Enneagram type, you can gain a deeper understanding of your core motivations and behaviors. This can help you identify areas where you need to focus your personal development efforts, such as improving your communication skills or emotional intelligence.

Research has shown that the Enneagram can be a valuable tool for self-development and personal growth (Lapid-Bogda, 2004). One study found that individuals who used the Enneagram as part of their personal development process reported significant improvements in their emotional intelligence, communication skills, and ability to work effectively with others (Ritz & Seville, 2016).

Each of the nine Enneagram types has a distinct set of core motivations and behaviors, which can help you understand why you think and act the way you do. For example, if you identify as an Enneagram Type One, also known as the Perfectionist, you may have a strong desire to do things right and a tendency to be critical of yourself and others. By understanding these traits, you can work on developing self-compassion, and learn to focus on progress, rather than perfection (Doyle, 2022a).

If you identify as an Enneagram Type Two, also known as the Helper, you may have a strong desire to help others and be liked by them. With this knowledge, you can work on setting healthy boundaries and taking care of your own needs (Doyle, 2022a).

Tips to Work On Your Strengths

One approach is to focus on developing your "*growth points*," which are the aspects of your Enneagram type that are less developed or underutilized (Don Richard Riso & Hudson, 1999). By focusing on these growth points, you can expand your range of behavior and develop new skills and strengths.

For example, if you are an Enneagram Type Five, also known as the Investigator, you may tend to withdraw from others and focus on your own thoughts and ideas. Your growth point may be to develop more connection with others, and to learn to express your ideas and feelings more openly. By intentionally working on these areas, you can become more well-rounded and effective in your personal and professional life.

Another approach is to focus on developing your "*wings*," which are the adjacent Enneagram types that influence your behavior (Don Richard Riso & Hudson, 1999). For example, if you are an Enneagram Type Two, also known as the Helper, your wings are either Type One, the Perfectionist, or Type Three, the Achiever. By focusing on the positive traits of your wings, such as the Perfectionist's attention to detail, or the Achiever's drive and ambition, you can develop new strengths and expand your range of behavior.

Research has shown that using the Enneagram in this way can lead to significant improvements in personal growth and well-being (Ritz & Seville, 2016). By focusing on your growth points and wings and intentionally working on developing your strengths, you can become more self-aware and effective in your personal and professional life.

Tips to Overcome Your Weaknesses

In addition to developing your strengths, the Enneagram can also be used to identify and overcome your weaknesses. By gaining a deeper understanding of your Enneagram type and the patterns of behavior that result from it, you can work to overcome negative behaviors and improve your overall well-being.

One way to do this is to focus on your "*stress point,*" which is the Enneagram type that you tend to adopt when you are under stress (Don Richard Riso & Hudson, 1999). When you are in a state of stress, you may exhibit behaviors that are unhealthy or counterproductive. By identifying your stress point and learning to recognize when you are in a state of stress, you can work to overcome these negative behaviors and return to a more healthy state.

For example, if you are an Enneagram Type One, also known as the Perfectionist, your stress point may be Type Four, the Individualist. When you are under stress, you may become more emotional, withdrawing from others. By learning to recognize when you are in a state of stress and focusing on healthy coping mechanisms, such as exercise or meditation, you can overcome these negative behaviors, and return to a more balanced state.

Another approach is to focus on your "*blind spot,*" which is the aspect of your personality that you may be unaware of, or may not fully understand (Don Richard Riso & Hudson, 1999). By identifying your blind spot and working to become more aware of it, you can overcome negative behaviors and become more well-rounded.

For example, if you are an Enneagram Type Seven, also known as the Enthusiast, your blind spot may be the negative impact that your impulsivity and restlessness can have on others. By working to become more aware of these negative behaviors, and developing strategies to control them, you can become more effective in your personal and professional relationships.

Research has shown that using the Enneagram in this way can lead to significant improvements in personal growth and well-being (Grahek, 2018). By focusing on your stress point and blind spot and intentionally working on overcoming your weaknesses, you can become more self-aware and effective in your personal and professional life.

One of the *key benefits of the Enneagram is that it promotes self-acceptance and self-compassion*. By recognizing that each Enneagram type has its own unique strengths and challenges, you can begin to embrace your own personality and stop comparing yourself to others. Instead of feeling shame or guilt about your weaknesses, you can view them as opportunities for growth and learning.

Another benefit of the Enneagram is that it *promotes empathy and understanding towards others*. By gaining a deeper understanding of the motivations and behaviors of people with different Enneagram types, you can become more effective in your personal and professional relationships. You can learn to communicate more effectively, collaborate more productively, and resolve conflicts more peacefully.

Finally, it's worth noting that *the Enneagram is not a magic solution to all of life's problems.* While it can be a powerful tool, it's important to remember that each individual is unique and complex, and that no personality system can fully capture the complexity of human nature. However, the Enneagram can help you identify patterns of behavior that may be holding you back, and provide a roadmap for personal transformation. By recognizing your patterns and working to break free from them, you can experience greater freedom and fulfillment in your life.

Chapter 15:
Using the Enneagram
for Personal Growth and Development

By discovering your Enneagram type and unpacking its implications, we can gain insight into ourselves and others, cultivate self-awareness, and develop healthier relationships. This chapter will guide you through the process of using the Enneagram for personal growth and development. Whether you're new to the Enneagram, or have been studying it for years, you'll find practical tips, exercises, and insights that can help you on your journey. *Throughout this chapter, we'll emphasize that the Enneagram is not a one-size-fits-all solution*, but rather a dynamic framework that can be adapted to your unique needs and goals.

Start With Understanding Your Personality Type

Investigate your core traits and tendencies. Now that you have reached this portion of the book, I am assuming that you know which Enneagram type you fall into. So, once you have identified that, it's crucial that you figure out the underlying behaviors and motivations that shape your personality.

Examine the wings and variations. You are already aware of the fact that every Enneagram type has its own set of distinctive traits, but each type has a certain degree of variability within it too. For example, in the previous chapters, you learned about "wings", adjacent Enneagram types that modify and influence your dominant type. Then there are also subtypes, or "instinctual variants", that reflect different expressions of your Enneagram type based on your primary survival strategy. By now you should be researching these aspects of your personality to get a better grasp of what your Enneagram means.

Recognize your levels of development. The Enneagram is not just a static system of nine types, but a dynamic model that accounts for different levels of psychological health and growth. In the previous chapters, I have covered the levels of development in great detail and how each type can manifest at different stages of your life under different circumstances. Your task is to understand these different levels of development, so that you can understand your own patterns of behavior, and identify the areas in your life that qualify for personal growth.

Explore your integration and disintegration points. Each Enneagram type has two other types that it connects to through its "integration" and "disintegration" points. These points reveal the ways in which your type can expand or contract under stress or in times of growth. You need to understand how you can access the positive qualities of your integration point and avoid the pitfalls of your disintegration point, thus enhancing your personal development.

Embrace your unique path. Finally, it's important to remember that the Enneagram is a tool for self-discovery, not a prescriptive formula for personal growth. Hence, your personality type is only one facet of your identity. By integrating your Enneagram insights with other practices and perspectives, you can create a holistic approach to personal growth and development.

Identify Your Triggers and Patterns

One of the most powerful aspects of the Enneagram is its ability to help us recognize our unconscious patterns of behavior, including the triggers that set off our automatic reactions. By becoming more aware of our triggers and patterns, we can start to take more intentional and conscious actions, rather than simply reacting from a place of habit. For instance, if you're a Type Two, you might have a tendency to overextend yourself to help others, which can lead to burnout and resentment if you're not careful (Chestnut, 2013).

To recognize your triggers and patterns, it can be helpful to reflect on your past experiences, and identify recurring themes or situations that trigger strong emotional reactions or unhelpful behaviors. You might also pay attention to your physical sensations, such as tension in your body or racing thoughts, as these can be indicators of an impending trigger or pattern. Once you've identified your triggers and patterns, you can start to explore healthier responses and strategies for managing them.

One useful tool for recognizing triggers and patterns is the Enneagram's concept of the "holy ideas" and "virtues" associated with each type. These qualities represent the positive aspects of each type's underlying motivations and can serve as a guide for healthier behavior. For instance, if you're a Type Four, your holy idea is that you are inherently connected to all things, while your virtue is equanimity. By focusing on these qualities, you can shift your attention away from your triggers and towards more constructive and empowering behaviors (Don Richard Riso & Hudson, 1999).

In addition, working with a therapist or coach who is trained in the Enneagram can be a helpful way to deepen your understanding of your triggers and patterns and develop personalized strategies for growth.

Address Your Desires and Core Fears

At the heart of the Enneagram system are the core fears and desires that drive each type's behavior. By understanding these underlying motivations, you can gain insight into why you think, feel, and act the way you do. For instance, if you're a Type Five, you might have a deep fear of being overwhelmed or depleted, which can lead you to hoard resources and withdraw from social situations (Palmer, 1991).

To address your core fears and desires, it can be helpful to reflect on how they show up in your life and relationships. You might ask yourself questions like: What situations trigger my fear? What activities or experiences bring me a sense of satisfaction or fulfillment? By exploring these questions, you can start to develop a deeper awareness of your underlying motivations and how they impact your behavior.

One helpful tool for addressing core fears and desires is the Enneagram's concept of the "passions" and "fixations" associated with each type. These qualities represent the negative aspects of each type's underlying motivations and can help you recognize when you're getting caught up in unhelpful patterns of thought or behavior. For instance, if you're a Type Nine, your passion is sloth, which can manifest as a tendency to avoid conflict or prioritize others' needs over your own. By recognizing when you're slipping into a state of sloth, you can take steps to become more proactive and assertive in your life (Don Richard Riso & Hudson, 1999).

Develop Healthy Coping Mechanisms

One of the benefits of using the Enneagram for personal growth and development is that it can help you identify and develop healthier coping mechanisms. Each Enneagram type has its own set of strengths and weaknesses, and by recognizing these patterns, you can start to build more effective ways of coping with stress and adversity.

For instance, if you're a Type Three, you might have a tendency to push yourself to achieve at all costs, which can lead to burnout and a sense of disconnection from your true self (Chestnut, 2013). To develop healthier coping mechanisms, you might explore practices like mindfulness meditation, which can help you tune into your inner experience, and build resilience in the face of stress.

Another helpful tool for developing healthy coping mechanisms is the Enneagram's concept of the "wings" associated with each type. These qualities represent the traits that are adjacent to your core type and can serve as a source of support and balance. For instance, if you're a Type Six with a Five wing, you might lean on your analytical and problem-solving skills to navigate difficult situations (Don Richard Riso & Hudson, 1999).

In addition, working with a therapist or coach who is trained in the Enneagram can be a powerful way to develop healthier coping mechanisms. By exploring your type's unique strengths and challenges, you can identify concrete steps towards building resilience, improving your relationships, and achieving your goals. Therapists and coaches who use the Enneagram may also incorporate other evidence-based practices, such as cognitive-behavioral therapy or mindfulness-based stress reduction, to help you build a well-rounded toolkit for coping with life's challenges.

Continue Your Enneagram Journey

Continuing your Enneagram journey involves ongoing self-awareness and growth. Here are some ways to continue your Enneagram journey:

- Attend workshops and seminars: There are many workshops and seminars available that delve deeper into Enneagram theory and offer guidance on how to apply it to your personal growth and development. These events can help you gain a better understanding of your type and how to navigate your inner world.

- Read books: There are many books available on the Enneagram that offer insight into each type and how to work with the challenges and strengths associated with each. Reading Enneagram books can also help you deepen your understanding of the Enneagram system as a whole.

- Work with a coach or therapist: Working with a certified Enneagram coach or therapist can provide personalized guidance and support as you navigate your Enneagram journey. They can help you identify patterns and work through challenges, as well as offer tools and resources to help you continue your personal growth.

- Join a community: Joining an Enneagram community can provide support and encouragement as you continue your journey. Whether it's attending a local Enneagram meetup group or joining an online community, connecting with others who share your interest in the Enneagram can help you feel more connected and supported in your journey.

Developing new behaviors to replace old, unhelpful habits is key to finding personal freedom. While this process may take time, and there is no quick fix, the Enneagram can be a valuable tool for transformation. However, it is important to approach this process without judgment, recognizing that it may be challenging to let go of ingrained habits that have been developed over years. With patience and commitment, it is possible to create healthier habits and live a more fulfilling life.

ENNEAGRAM AND RELATIONSHIPS

Chapter 16:
Understanding and Relating to Others

As you already know, the Enneagram is a model of human personality that describes nine interconnected types, each with its own set of core motivations, fears, and desires. It is used not only as a tool for personal growth and self-awareness, but also as a means of understanding and relating to others.

The system is based on the idea that *each person has a dominant personality type* that influences their thoughts, feelings, and behaviors. This type is shaped by a combination of genetic, environmental, and cultural factors, and reflects the unique ways in which a person navigates the world around them.

Understanding the Enneagram can be helpful in relating to others because it provides a framework for understanding the underlying motivations and fears that drive people's behavior. By recognizing the different Enneagram types, we can gain insight into *why people act the way they do, and develop greater empathy and compassion for their struggles and challenges.*

One study found that individuals who completed an Enneagram-based training program reported increased self-awareness and a greater ability to understand and communicate with others (Abdel-Khalek, 2013). Another study found that the Enneagram was helpful in improving communication and teamwork in the workplace (Vidal & Gómez, 2016).

Overall, the Enneagram can be a useful tool for individuals and organizations seeking to improve interpersonal relationships, communication, and collaboration. By understanding and relating to others through the lens of the Enneagram, we can build stronger, more fulfilling connections with the people around us.

Developing Empathy and Compassion

The Enneagram provides a valuable tool for understanding behaviors that may irritate or frustrate us. For example, we may find it difficult to get along with overly competitive people, or those who dominate conversations. The Enneagram can help us understand the deeper motivations behind these behaviors, leading to greater compassion and mercy towards others. Rather than avoiding these behaviors, we can look at them with understanding and empathy.

As an example, I once worked with a colleague who constantly corrected others in front of clients. Initially, I assumed the person was simply trying to compete for their position. However, after learning their Enneagram type, which was Type One, I realized that the corrections were motivated by a desire for correctness, rather than malice or ambition. Understanding this helped me become more patient and sympathetic towards them.

The Enneagram is particularly useful for developing empathy towards others. I prefer to believe that empathy is the Enneagram's greatest feature. In addition to understanding others, the Enneagram can also help individuals understand themselves. By identifying the core motivations behind their behaviors, individuals can gain insight into their deepest desires and sins. This can help them address the root causes of their struggles, and seek growth, as you read in the previous chapters of this book.

Some people believe that Enneagram-type tests have drawbacks because of the potential to excuse behavior as "just how you are." I acknowledge that there is a tendency to utilize its behavioral explanations to avoid altering. A person of type 7 may utilize the Enneagram as a justification for reckless and shallow behavior. If someone points out the destructive potential of their habits, they may invoke their "enthusiast" label and dismiss legitimate warnings.

However, recognizing your greatest vulnerability can also be your greatest advantage. Type Nines are considered the Peacemaker. The downside of their personality type is avoiding conflict in order to have a perceived peaceful environment. However, when Type Nines recognize this tendency, they can serve as an important component in the community's healing.

At its most developed, the Nine can perceive tension, they also have the ability to assist people in addressing issues in a productive manner.

Learning to Integrate Enneagram in Your Interpersonal Interactions

Recognize the Enneagram type that others have. Recognizing Enneagram types in others can be a powerful tool for building stronger relationships and improving communication. By understanding someone's Enneagram type, you can tailor your communication style to better suit their needs, avoid misunderstandings, and build trust and empathy. One way to begin identifying someone's Enneagram type is to pay attention to their behavior patterns. Each type has its own set of behaviors that are associated with their core motivation (Brown, 2023). For example, a Type One is often perfectionistic and detail-oriented, while a Type Two is often focused on pleasing others and meeting their needs.

Another way to identify someone's Enneagram type is to listen to the language they use to describe themselves and others (Lee, 2015). Each type has its own language and way of seeing the world. For example, a Type Four may use phrases like "I feel so misunderstood" or "no one truly gets me," while a Type Eight may use language that is more forceful and direct. By paying attention to the language someone uses, you can get a better sense of their Enneagram type.

It is important to note that identifying someone's Enneagram type should not be used as a way to label or stereotype them. Rather, it should be used as a tool to deepen your understanding of them and their behavior (Lee, 2015).

Manage conflicts with understanding of the Enneagram. Managing conflict can be tough—and I can't agree more with you on that—but having an understanding of the Enneagram can help to navigate difficult situations with more empathy and understanding. Here are some ways to use the Enneagram to manage conflict:

- When conflict arises, take a step back and try to identify the other person's Enneagram type. This can help you understand their perspective and motivations, which can help to defuse the situation.

- Each Enneagram type has their own communication style, and understanding this can help you communicate more effectively during conflict. For example, Type Nines tend to avoid conflict, while Type Eights are more confrontational.

- Conflict often arises due to underlying issues that have not been addressed. By understanding each person's Enneagram type, you can better understand what these underlying issues might be. For example, a Type One may be driven by a desire for perfection, while a Type Four may struggle with feelings of inadequacy.

Using Enneagram understanding in daily life involves applying the insights gained from knowing one's own and other's Enneagram types to improve personal and interpersonal relationships. This can include paying attention to one's own patterns of behavior and identifying how they relate to one's Enneagram type, as well as recognizing the Enneagram types of others in order to understand and empathize with their motivations and actions, all of which you have already learned in this chapter and now, you need to start applying them in your own life.

Chapter 17:
Understanding the Enneagram
in Teams and Organizations

Understanding the Enneagram in teams and organizations can be a game-changer when it comes to *building successful and harmonious work environments*. The Enneagram is a powerful personality typing tool that can help individuals gain a deeper understanding of themselves, and their colleagues. It provides a framework for identifying and working with personality traits that can enhance or hinder individual and team performance.

In this chapter, we will explore the Enneagram system and its applications in the context of teams and organizations. By the end of this chapter, you will have a solid understanding of how the Enneagram can be used to enhance team dynamics, foster communication, and improve performance in the workplace. You will also gain insight into strategies of successful Enneagram implementations and understand how to avoid common misconceptions that can undermine its effectiveness.

Benefits of Enneagram in the Workplace Setting

The Enneagram offers numerous benefits to teams and organizations when used as a tool for understanding individual and team dynamics.

- The Enneagram provides a common language for discussing personality types and traits, allowing team members to communicate more effectively and work together more cohesively. According to a study by Palmer, the Enneagram can help team members develop greater self-awareness and empathy for others, leading to improved communication and collaboration (Palmer, 1991).

- The Enneagram can enhance individual and team performance by providing insights into motivation, decision-making, and behavior patterns. In a study by Kark, Shamir, and Chen, the Enneagram was found to be a useful tool for leadership development, providing leaders with a greater understanding of their own strengths and weaknesses, and how to better manage their teams (Kark et al., 2003).

- The Enneagram can be used to create more effective teams by balancing individual strengths and weaknesses.

As noted by Lapid-Bogda, the Enneagram can help teams identify gaps in skills and knowledge, allowing for the creation of more well-rounded teams (Lapid-Bogda, 2004). By leveraging the unique strengths of each team member, the Enneagram can lead to higher levels of team performance.

- The Enneagram can facilitate personal and professional growth by providing a roadmap for self-improvement. By understanding their Enneagram type and corresponding strengths and weaknesses, team members can identify areas for personal and professional development. This can lead to greater job satisfaction, higher levels of engagement, and improved performance (Rickerd, 2019).

Thus, by leveraging the insights provided by the Enneagram, teams and organizations can build stronger, more cohesive teams and create a more positive and productive work environment.

Implementation Strategies

Implementing the Enneagram in teams and organizations requires careful planning and consideration. Here are some strategies for successfully integrating the Enneagram into your team or organizational culture:

Define the purpose and goals. Before implementing the Enneagram, it's important to clearly define the purpose and goals of using it in your organization. This could include improving communication, building stronger teams, or developing leadership skills. Defining the purpose and goals will help ensure that everyone involved is aligned and working towards a common objective.

Educate your team. Introducing the Enneagram to your team requires education and training. Consider offering workshops or training sessions to help team members understand the Enneagram system and their own Enneagram type. This will help create a shared language and understanding of the Enneagram within your organization.

Encourage self-discovery. Encourage team members to explore and discover their own Enneagram type through self-reflection and assessment tools. This can be done individually, or as a team-building activity. Encouraging self-discovery will help team members develop greater self-awareness and empathy for others.

Create a safe and supportive environment. Implementing the Enneagram can be a sensitive and personal topic. Creating a safe and supportive environment where team members feel comfortable discussing their Enneagram type and related issues is crucial to success. Consider setting ground rules for discussions, such as confidentiality and respect.

Address resistance and misconceptions. Some team members may be resistant or skeptical about the Enneagram. Addressing misconceptions and concerns upfront can help mitigate resistance and build buy-in. Consider addressing common misconceptions, such as the Enneagram being a personality test, and clarify that it is a tool for self-discovery and personal growth.

Enhance team dynamics. Once team members have a better understanding of the Enneagram system, use it to enhance team dynamics. For example, identify each team member's Enneagram type and corresponding strengths and weaknesses, and use this knowledge to build more effective teams, delegate tasks, and provide feedback.

Make the Enneagram part of your organizational culture. Finally, to maximize the benefits of the Enneagram, make it part of your organizational culture. This can include incorporating the Enneagram into performance evaluations, leadership development programs, and team-building activities.

Learn to Avoid the Pitfalls

While the Enneagram can be a powerful tool for improving team dynamics and organizational culture, there are also some common pitfalls and misconceptions to be aware of. In this section, we'll explore these pitfalls and offer some friendly advice on how to avoid them.

Pitfall 1: Enneagram Typing Stereotypes

One common pitfall is falling into the trap of Enneagram typing stereotypes. It's important to remember that the Enneagram is a tool for self-discovery, not a rigid categorization system. Avoid making assumptions about team members based on their Enneagram type, and instead use it as a starting point for understanding their unique strengths and weaknesses.

Friendly Advice: Encourage team members to embrace their Enneagram type as a way to better understand themselves and their colleagues. Remind them that the Enneagram is just one aspect of their personality, and that everyone is unique.

Pitfall 2: Lack of Enneagram Education and Training

Another pitfall is not providing adequate education and training on the Enneagram. Without proper understanding and training, team members may misinterpret or misuse the Enneagram, leading to confusion and potential conflict.

Friendly Advice: Offer Enneagram education and training to team members to ensure they have a solid understanding of the system and how to use it effectively. Encourage open communication and questions to clarify any misunderstandings.

Pitfall 3: Enneagram Used as a Weapon

Another pitfall is using the Enneagram as a weapon, such as using it to criticize or judge team members. This can lead to hurt feelings and damaged relationships.

Friendly Advice: Remind team members that the Enneagram is a tool for understanding and empathy, not criticism or judgment. Encourage them to use the Enneagram to better understand and appreciate the unique strengths and perspectives of their colleagues.

Tips For Incorporating Enneagram Training and Development

Here are some tips for incorporating Enneagram training and development into your team or organization:

- Customize training: Enneagram training should be customized to your team or organization's unique needs and goals. Consider incorporating real-life examples and exercises to make the training more engaging and relevant.
- Provide ongoing support: Enneagram development is an ongoing process, and team members may need ongoing support to fully integrate the Enneagram into their work and personal lives. Consider providing ongoing coaching or follow-up training sessions to reinforce the Enneagram principles.
- Encourage open communication: Enneagram development requires open and honest communication. Encourage team members to be open and honest about their Enneagram types, and how they impact their work and relationships.
- Lead by example: Enneagram training starts at the top. Encourage leaders to model Enneagram principles in their work and relationships, and to actively encourage their team members to embrace the Enneagram as a tool for growth and development.
- Use Enneagram typing as a starting point, not a label: Enneagram typing should be used as a starting point for self-awareness and growth, not as a label that defines a

person. Encourage team members to embrace their Enneagram type as a tool for growth and development, rather than as a fixed characteristic.

- Integrate Enneagram development into performance management: Consider integrating Enneagram development into performance management processes, such as goal-setting and performance reviews. This can help team members apply Enneagram principles to their work and track their progress over time.

- Consider Enneagram diversity: While Enneagram development can offer many benefits, it's important to recognize that individuals may have different levels of comfort with the Enneagram, or may not find it relevant to their work. Be mindful of Enneagram diversity, and ensure that training and development opportunities are inclusive and respectful of all team members.

- Encourage collaboration and feedback: Encourage team members to collaborate and provide feedback to one another as they apply Enneagram principles to their work and relationships. This can help team members learn from one another and deepen their understanding of the Enneagram.

In conclusion, while the Enneagram can be a valuable tool for teams and organizations, it's important to be aware of the potential pitfalls and misconceptions. By avoiding Enneagram typing stereotypes, providing adequate education and training, viewing the Enneagram as a tool for growth rather than a label, and using it to promote empathy rather than criticism, teams and organizations can maximize the benefits of the Enneagram and achieve greater success.

Chapter 18:
Using the Enneagram in
Relationships and Communication

Are you hearing the word 'Enneagram' too much nowadays? Well, that's probably because it has gained quite the popularity in recent years as a tool for personal growth and self-awareness. However, the Enneagram can also be a valuable resource for enhancing our relationships with others, both in romantic and family settings. In this chapter, we will explore how the Enneagram can be used to improve relationships and communication.

Using the Enneagram to Improve Communication in Relationships

Have you ever felt like you just can't seem to get through to your partner or loved one, no matter how hard you try? Maybe you feel like you're speaking a different language, or that they're just not getting what you're trying to say. Well, you're not alone! Communication can be tricky, and sometimes it feels like we're not speaking the same language as the people closest to us.

That's where the Enneagram comes in. The Enneagram is a powerful tool that can help us better understand ourselves and others. You have already learned about each type in depth in the previous part of this book, but let's take a look at how each Enneagram type communicates and some tips for how to communicate with them effectively:

Type One—The Perfectionist: Ones tend to communicate with clarity and precision, but they can also come across as critical and judgmental. To communicate effectively with a One, try to focus on the positive, and be specific with your feedback (Rimland, 2019).

Type Two—The Helper: Twos are warm, empathetic, and great listeners, but they can also be prone to people-pleasing and neglecting their own needs. To communicate effectively with a Two, make sure to express your appreciation for their efforts, and encourage them to take care of themselves too (Yuan, 2019).

Type Three—The Achiever: Threes are confident, goal-oriented, and great at multitasking, but they can also be competitive and overly focused on success. To communicate effectively with a Three, be direct and concise, and make sure to acknowledge their hard work (Rimland, 2019).

Type Four—The Individualist: Fours are creative, introspective, and value authenticity, but they can also be moody and overly focused on their emotions. To communicate effectively with a Four, be empathetic, and show interest in their feelings and experiences (Yuan, 2019).

Type Five—The Investigator: Fives are analytical, insightful, and value privacy, but they can also be withdrawn and emotionally detached. To communicate effectively with a Five, be patient, give them space when they need it, and ask for their input and expertise (Christian, 2020).

Type Six—The Loyalist: Sixes are loyal, responsible, and great at anticipating potential problems, but they can also be anxious and prone to self-doubt. To communicate effectively with a Six, be supportive and offer reassurance when they need it, and be clear and direct in your communication (Rimland, 2019).

Type Seven—The Enthusiast: Sevens are optimistic, adventurous, and love to have fun, but they can also be impulsive and distractible. To communicate effectively with a Seven, keep things light and positive, and allow them room to explore new ideas and experiences (Yuan, 2019).

Type Eight—The Challenger: Eights are confident, assertive, and value strength and control, but they can also be confrontational and intimidating. To communicate effectively with an Eight, be honest and direct, but also show respect for their boundaries and opinions (Christian, 2020).

Type Nine—The Peacemaker: Nines are easygoing, diplomatic, and great at finding common ground, but they can also be passive and indecisive. To communicate effectively with a Nine, be patient, avoid putting pressure on them, and make sure to listen actively to their perspective (Rimland, 2019).

By understanding each Enneagram type's communication style and adapting our approach accordingly, we can improve our communication and build stronger relationships.

The Enneagram and Love Languages

Love is a universal language, but did you know that each person has their own unique way of expressing and receiving love? These love languages were first introduced by Dr. Gary Chapman and include acts of service, quality time, words of affirmation, physical touch, and receiving gifts. Knowing your partner's love language can be a game-changer in your relationship, and when combined with the Enneagram, it can be a powerful tool for enhancing your connection and communication.

Let's take a look at how each Enneagram type's love language tends to manifest, and how you can speak your partner's love language more effectively:

Type One—The Perfectionist: Ones tend to express love through acts of service, such as doing chores, or running errands for their partner. If your partner is a One, try to show your appreciation for their efforts and help out, either around the house or with tasks they find important (Strong, 2020).

Type Two—The Helper: Twos express love through spending quality time, such as doing things together or supporting their partner's goals. If your partner is a Two, make sure to give them your undivided attention, and offer your support and encouragement (The Enneagram and Love Languages, 2022).

Type Three—The Achiever: Threes express love through quality time and words of affirmation, such as praise and recognition for their achievements. If your partner is a Three, make sure to acknowledge their hard work, and make time for shared activities and experiences (Shatto, 2020).

Type Four—The Individualist: Fours express love by doing things such as sharing deep conversations or expressing their emotions. If your partner is a Four, some things that you can do are making sure to validate their feelings and showing interest in their unique perspective (The Enneagram and Love Languages, 2022).

Type Five—The Investigator: Fives show their love by sharing their knowledge or doing things together. If your partner is a Five, make sure to respect their need for solitude and give them space when they need it, but also show appreciation for their contributions (Strong, 2020).

Type Six—The Loyalist: Sixes express love through acts of service and words of affirmation, such as providing support and reassurance. If your partner is a Six, make sure to show your commitment and dependability, and provide a sense of safety and security (Shatto, 2020).

Type Seven—The Enthusiast: Sevens express love through quality time and physical touch, such as shared adventures and playful affection. If your partner is a Seven, make sure to join them in their fun, and show your love through playful gestures and physical affection (The Enneagram and Love Languages, 2022).

Type Eight—The Challenger: Eights show their love through acts like protective gestures and taking care of their partner's needs. If your partner is an Eight, make sure to show your support and appreciation for their strength and protectiveness (Strong, 2020).

Type Nine—The Peacemaker: Last but definitely not the least, Nines express love through shared experiences and providing a sense of peace and stability. If your partner is a Nine, make sure to show your interest and attention, and help them feel heard and understood (Shatto, 2020).

With the Enneagram and love languages as your guide, you can build a stronger, more loving relationship.

Overcoming Relationship Challenges With the Enneagram

Every relationship goes through its own share of ups and downs. Here are some common relationship challenges, and how the Enneagram can help you overcome them:

Communication breakdown. Misunderstandings and communication breakdowns can happen in any relationship. I can't stress this enough, but by understanding your own and your partner's Enneagram type, you can identify your communication style, and adapt it to better communicate with each other. For example, if you're a Type One, and your partner is a Type Eight, you may need to be more direct and assertive in your communication style, while your partner may need to work on listening more actively.

Different perspectives. Each Enneagram type has its own unique perspective on the world, which can sometimes clash with your partner's. By understanding your partner's perspective and learning to appreciate their unique strengths and challenges, you can build greater empathy and understanding in your relationship. This can help you overcome differences and find common ground.

Emotional triggers. Every Enneagram type has its own set of emotional triggers and patterns of behavior. By recognizing your own and your partner's triggers, you can avoid getting caught up in reactive patterns, and instead work together to address underlying issues. For example, if you're a Type Four, and your partner is a Type Nine, you may need to be more aware of your tendency to withdraw or become moody, while your partner may need to work on expressing their needs more assertively.

Different needs and expectations. Each Enneagram type has its own set of needs and expectations in a relationship. By understanding your own and your partner's needs, you can work together to create a more fulfilling and satisfying relationship. For example, if you're a Type Two, and your partner is a Type Five, you may need to communicate your need for emotional connection and support, while your partner may need to express their need for space and independence.

Remember that when it comes to relationship challenges, the Enneagram is definitely not a one-size-fits-all solution. But, what it can do is that it can help you start communicating in a more open and honest manner.

Can the Enneagram Help Strengthen Parent-Child Relationships Too?

It's true that parenting is one of the most rewarding phases in life, but, at the same time, it can be one of the most challenging ones too. Here are some ways the Enneagram can help you strengthen your parent-child relationship:

Understanding your child's perspective. Each Enneagram type has its own unique perspective on the world, and by understanding your child's type, you can gain insight into their needs, strengths, and challenges. This understanding can help you connect with your child on a deeper level and be more empathetic and supportive of their growth and development.

Tailoring your parenting style. Each Enneagram type has its own set of needs and expectations, and by understanding your own type and your child's type, you can tailor your parenting style to better meet their needs. For example, if you're a Type One, and your child is a Type Seven, you may need to work on being more flexible and spontaneous to meet your child's need for excitement and variety.

Recognizing triggers and patterns. Every Enneagram type has its own set of triggers and patterns of behavior, and by recognizing these patterns in yourself and your child, you can avoid reactive patterns, instead working together to address underlying issues. For example, if you're a Type Eight, and your child is a Type Four, you may need to be aware of your tendency to be more forceful and direct, while your child may need more space and sensitivity to express their emotions.

Building communication. Effective communication is essential to building a strong parent-child relationship, and the Enneagram can help you understand your communication style and adapt it to better connect with your child. By speaking your child's Enneagram language, you can help them feel understood and valued, which can lead to a more positive and supportive relationship.

In conclusion, the Enneagram is a valuable tool for building stronger and more fulfilling relationships, whether with romantic partners, family members, or children.

Conclusion

In conclusion, the Enneagram provides a unique approach to understanding personality types, not only focusing on how each type behaves when healthy and balanced, but also on how they can return to a state of ascendance when they become unbalanced. By recognizing that all people have the components of every type within them, the Enneagram offers a path towards greater self-awareness and personal growth. This growth involves returning to emotional, physical, and intellectual balance, and learning how to navigate conflict in a more balanced and appropriate way. The key to ascendance lies in acknowledging our strengths, as well as our weaknesses, and learning how to overcome them. Whether you're overly assertive, compliant, or withdrawn, the Enneagram offers practical tools and exercises to help you become more balanced, and live a more fulfilling life.

Furthermore, the Enneagram offers a powerful tool for personal and spiritual growth by revealing our unconscious patterns and the motivations behind our behavior. By understanding these patterns and motivations, we can break free from our limited perspectives, and transform our lives. The Enneagram helps us to understand our deepest fears, desires, and motivations, and how they influence our thoughts, emotions, and actions. This knowledge allows us to cultivate greater self-awareness, compassion, and acceptance, and to develop more fulfilling and harmonious relationships with ourselves and others. The Enneagram is not just a personality typing system, but a holistic approach to self-discovery and personal development that can lead to greater happiness, fulfillment, and inner peace.

If you are someone who identifies as a Type One, you might often struggle with perfectionism, and can become overly critical of myself and others. However, you will see that when you are in a healthy and balanced state, you can use your attention to detail and high standards to make positive changes in your life and the world around you.

On the other hand, when you are in an unhealthy state, you may become rigid and inflexible, causing you to miss out on opportunities for growth and connection. By recognizing your tendencies and working to stay balanced, you can use your strengths to your advantage while avoiding the pitfalls of your weaknesses.

Similarly, a friend of mine who identifies as a Type Nine often struggles with assertiveness and standing up for themselves.

However, they've learned that when they're in a healthy and balanced state, they can use their gift for empathy and understanding to create harmony and bring people together.

But when they're in an unhealthy state, they may become complacent and avoid conflict, causing them to miss out on important opportunities for growth and not standing up for what they believe in. By recognizing their tendencies and working to stay balanced, they can use their strengths to build connections while still advocating for themselves and others when necessary.

Figuring out your Enneagram type can be a little tricky, but don't worry, I've got some tips to help you out. It's important to approach the process in the right way. Rather than focusing on your strengths, or what you aspire to be, try to identify the type that you would be most embarrassed to admit you are. It can be tough to confront your flaws, but it's the first step in repairing them and living a more authentic life.

The Enneagram is a powerful tool for understanding how your life experiences have shaped you and identifying areas for growth. While it may be tempting to look at your behaviors and try to decide your type based on those, it's important to consider the motivations and experiences behind those actions. Remember that some behaviors may have been learned from other types or from your environment, so they may not be an accurate reflection of your type.

It's also important to be aware of the possibility of confusing your direction of integration with your actual type. To avoid this, think about what your best self looks like, and what your worst self looks like. Your best self should align with your type or the direction of integration from your type, while your worst self will align with your type or the direction of disintegration.

So, don't get discouraged if identifying your type feels challenging at first. With a little reflection and honesty, you'll be able to unlock a wealth of insights about yourself and move towards a more fulfilling life.

While some may turn to tests to identify their Enneagram type, I have found them to be less accurate than a thorough reading of all the type descriptions. By focusing on the flaws within each type, you can better identify which one resonates with your own personal demons and learn how to banish them. Even if you think you already know your type, it is worth learning about all the types and their best and worst qualities, as these aspects are present in all of us to some extent. Ultimately, expanding your knowledge of the Enneagram can provide valuable insights into the motivations of others and help foster greater understanding and compassion.

References

Abdel-Khalek, A. M. (2013). The Enneagram of personality: A validity study in an Arabic-speaking sample. *Psychological Reports, 112*(2), 397–414. https://doi.org/10.2466/02.09.PR0.112.2.397-414

Alderson, J. (2022, July 26). *Enneagram type 8: So assertive.* So Syncd. https://www.sosyncd.com/enneagram-type-8/

Alexander, M., & Schnipke, B. (2020). The Enneagram: A primer for psychiatry residents. *American Journal of Psychiatry Residents' Journal, 15*(3), 2–5. https://doi.org/10.1176/appi.ajp-rj.2020.150301

Bayside Church. (2016, December 30). *How to change your life using the Enneagram — Part 1: The nine types and deadly passions.* Medium. https://medium.com/@BaysideChurch/how-to-use-the-enneagram-find-your-number-and-transform-your-life-c7dc3649b897

Belle, E. (2020, June 30). *How does the Enneagram work and how useful is it?* Healthline. https://www.healthline.com/health/mental-health/how-does-the-enneagram-work

Bernes, M. (n.d.). *What are the nine Enneagram types? How to interpret them?* www.makipeople.com. Retrieved May 17, 2023, from https://www.makipeople.com/resources/how-to-interpret-nine-enneagram-types

Booth, J. (2022, April 29). *The 9 Enneagram personality types: Strengths, weaknesses and more.* Forbes Health. https://www.forbes.com/health/mind/enneagram-types/

Brand, S. (2021, February 20). *An Enneagram guide for self-care: Type 1.* Heights Family Counseling. https://heightsfamilycounseling.com/blog/2021/2/20/an-enneagram-guide-for-self-care-type-1

Brown, S. (2023). Studying communication competence level and the Enneagram type. *Journal of Student Research at Indiana University East, 5*(1).

https://scholarworks.iu.edu/journals/index.php/jsriue/article/view/357 44

Cain, S. (2016). *Quiet power : the secret strengths of introverted kids.* New York Puffin Books United States Dial Books For Young Readers.

Carroll, J. S., & Ivanoff, S. D. (2016). Increasing self-awareness through self-discovery: A grounded theory study of women leaders. *Journal of Leadership Education, 15*(2), 139–151. https://doi.org/10.12806/V15/I2/R6

Cherry, K. (2019, July). *What is the Enneagram of personality?* Verywell Mind. https://www.verywellmind.com/the-enneagram-of-personality-4691757

Chestnut, B. (2013). *The complete Enneagram.* She Writes Press.

Chestnut, B. (2021). *The Enneagram.* Beatrice Chestnut. https://www.beatricechestnut.com/enneagram

Christian, K. (2020, January 29). *How to cultivate healthier relationships based on your Enneagram type.* The Good Trade. https://www.thegoodtrade.com/features/enneagram-in-relationships/

Christian, K. (2021, January 8). *What are Enneagram types?* The Good Trade. https://www.thegoodtrade.com/features/what-are-enneagram-types/

Cloete, D. (2010). *Origins and history of the Enneagram.* Integrative9.com. https://www.integrative9.com/enneagram/history/

Cloete, D. (2022, April 6). *Nine holy ideas of the Enneagram.* Integrative9. https://www.integrative9.com/media/articles/51/The-Enneagram-of-Holy-Ideas

Don Richard Riso, & Hudson, R. (1999). *Wisdom of the Enneagram: The complete guide to psychological and spiritual growth for the nine personality types.* Bantam.

Doyle, E. (2022a, April 30). *A helpful guide to the Enneagram motivations of all 9 types.* Enneagram Gift. https://enneagramgift.com/enneagram-motivations/

Doyle, E. (2022b, June 1). *Enneagram type 8 identity + notorious traits of the Challenger.* Enneagram Gifts. https://enneagramgift.com/enneagram-type-8/

Doyle, E. (2022c, November 14). *Enneagram 9: The Peacemaker.* Cloverleaf. https://cloverleaf.me/blog/enneagram-type-9-the-peacemaker/

Emmons, R. A., & McCullough, M. E. (2003). Counting blessings versus burdens: An experimental investigation of gratitude and subjective well-being in daily life. *Journal of Personality and Social Psychology, 84*(2), 377–389. https://doi.org/10.1037/0022-3514.84.2.377

Enneagram centers of intelligence. (2020, January 21). Enneagram Explained. https://enneagramexplained.com/enneagram-centers-of-intelligence/

Enneagram type 3: The Achiever. (2021, July 20). Enneagram Explained. https://enneagramexplained.com/enneagram-3-the-achiever/

Enneagram type 4 – The Individualist. (2021, October 28). Enneagramuniverse.com. https://enneagramuniverse.com/enneagram/learn/enneagram-types/enneagram-type-4-the-individualist/

Enneagram type 7. (2022, October 21). Www.personalitydata.org. https://www.personalitydata.org/enneagram/type-7

Enneagram type 7 - The Adventurer. (n.d.). Www.crystalknows.com. https://www.crystalknows.com/enneagram/type-7

Enneagram type 8 description. (n.d.). David N. Daniels, M.D. Retrieved May 17, 2023, from https://drdaviddaniels.com/type-8/

Francis, A., & Singletary, J. (2022). *The Enneagram and communication styles.* https://baylor-ir.tdl.org/bitstream/handle/2104/11826/alex_francis1_honorsthesis%20.pdf?sequence=1

Grahek, M. (2018). The Enneagram: An empirical study of its factor structure. *Journal of Adult Development, 25*(3), 153–161. https://doi.org/10.1007/s10804-018-9287-6

Hook, J. N., Hall, T. W., Davis, D. E., Van Tongeren, D. R., & Conner, M. (2020). The Enneagram: A systematic review of the literature and directions for future research. *Journal of Clinical Psychology, 77*(4), 865–883. https://doi.org/10.1002/jclp.23097

How the Enneagram system works. (2014). The Enneagram Institute. https://www.enneagraminstitute.com/how-the-enneagram-system-works

James, J. (2021, November 7). *The existential emptiness of the Enneagram type 3. The 3 in* Me. https://medium.com/the-3-in-me/the-existential-emptiness-of-the-enneagram-type-3-ee84a9c50c49

Kark, R., Shamir, B., & Chen, G. (2003). The two faces of transformational leadership: Empowerment and dependency. *Journal of Applied Psychology, 88*(2), 246–255. https://doi.org/10.1037/0021-9010.88.2.246

Lapid-Bogda, G. (2004). *Bringing out the best in yourself at work.* McGraw Hill Professional.

Lee, M.-R. (2015). A study on the effects of Enneagram group counseling on nursing students. *International Journal of Bio-Science and Bio-Technology, 7*(5), 235–246. https://doi.org/10.14257/ijbsbt.2015.7.5.22

Maitri, S. (2000). *The spiritual dimension of the Enneagram.* Penguin.

McLeod, S. (2022). *Maslow's hierarchy of needs.* Simply Psychology. https://www.simplypsychology.org/maslow.html

Mukherjee, C. (2021, November 12). *All about enneagram 7 personality types – the Enthusiast.* ThePleasantPersonality. https://thepleasantpersonality.com/enneagram-type-7/

Mukherjee, C. (2023, March 2). *Enneagram 8 personality description – an energetic challenger.* ThePleasantPersonality. https://thepleasantpersonality.com/enneagram-8-personality-description/

Owens, M. (2019, August 8). *Enneagram type 1: The perfectionist.* Truity. https://www.truity.com/enneagram/personality-type-1-perfectionist

Palmer, H. (1991). *The Enneagram : understanding yourself and the others in your life.* HarperOne.

Personality type: Six – the Loyalist or Skeptic. (n.d.). Www.theworldcounts.com. Retrieved May 17, 2023, from https://www.theworldcounts.com/purpose/enneagram-number-6-personality-type-six-loyalist

Regan, S. (2021, July 8). *Are you an enneagram type4? Here's everything you should know.* Mindbodygreen. https://www.mindbodygreen.com/articles/enneagram-type-4-traits-strengths-compatibility-and-more

Rickerd, G. (2019, November 23). *Enneagram in the workplace: Using your type to your advantage.* Atomic Spin. https://spin.atomicobject.com/2019/11/23/enneagram-in-the-workplace/

Rimland, A. (2019, September 12). *How the Enneagram can improve your relationships.* Thrive Couple & Family Counseling Services. https://thrivefamilyservices.com/enneagram-improve-relationships/

Ritz, E. M., & Seville, C. (2016). The Enneagram: A model for enhancing teamwork in the workplace. *Journal of Management Development, 35*(2), 217–228. https://doi.org/10.1108/JMD-08-2014-0113

Roberts, B. W., Lejuez, C., Krueger, R. F., Richards, J. M., & Hill, P. L. (2014). What is conscientiousness and how can it be assessed? *Developmental Psychology, 50*(5), 1315–1330. https://doi.org/10.1037/a0031109

Robledo, I. (2022, March 16). *Enneagram 5 in stress & growth* . Making Mindfulness Fun. https://www.makingmindfulnessfun.com/enneagram-5-stress-growth/

Roulo, L. (2021, January 28). *Modern twists to the ancient Enneagram: How the personality system has changed over the last 20 years.* Truity. https://www.truity.com/blog/modern-twists-ancient-enneagram-how-personality-system-has-changed-over-last-20-years

Sarikas, C. (2020, December 23). *Enneagram type 7: The Enthusiast.* Blog.prepscholar.com. https://blog.prepscholar.com/enneagram-type-7-careers-relationships

Schirm, A. (2022, November 22). *Enneagram Two health tips - the ultimate guide.* The Living Well. https://thelivingwell.com/enneagram-two-health-tips-the-ultimate-guide/

Shatto, R. (2020, October 8). *Here's what your Enneagram type says about your love language.* Elite Daily. https://www.elitedaily.com/p/heres-what-your-enneagram-type-says-about-your-love-language-37937360

Storm, S. (2020, August 6). *Integration, disintegration and your Enneagram type.* Psychology Junkie. https://www.psychologyjunkie.com/enneagram-integration-disintegration/

Strong, R. (2020, August 5). *Here's what your Enneagram type says about your love language.* Elite Daily. https://www.elitedaily.com/p/your-enneagram-type-love-language-probably-are-in-sync-32180244

Sutin, A. R., Costa, P. T., Wethington, E., & Eaton, W. (2010). Turning points and lessons learned: Stressful life events and personality trait development across middle adulthood. *Psychology and Aging, 25*(3), 524–533. https://doi.org/10.1037/a0018751

The Enneagram and love languages. (2022, April 8). Enneagram Explained. https://enneagramexplained.com/the-enneagram-and-love-languages/

The Enneagram Institute. (n.d.-a). *Type Eight.* The Enneagram Institute. https://www.enneagraminstitute.com/type-8

The Enneagram Institute. (n.d.-b). *Type Seven.* The Enneagram Institute. https://www.enneagraminstitute.com/type-7

The Enneagram Institute. (2014a). *Type Six.* The Enneagram Institute. https://www.enneagraminstitute.com/type-6

The Enneagram Institute. (2014b). *Traditional Enneagram (History).* The Enneagram Institute. https://www.enneagraminstitute.com/the-traditional-enneagram

The Enneagram Institute. (2021). *Type Nine.* The Enneagram Institute. https://www.enneagraminstitute.com/type-9

The Enneagram model explained and why it isn't always a good idea. (n.d.). Www.bestenneagramtest.com. Retrieved May 14, 2023, from https://www.bestenneagramtest.com/blog/the-enneagram-model-explained-and-why-it-isn-t-always-a-good-idea-to-take-it

The Enneagram type 9: The Peacemaker. (2022, September 8). Www.traitlab.com. https://www.traitlab.com/blog/enneagram-type-9

The nine Enneagram types [Complete Descriptions]. (n.d.). Personalitypath.com. https://personalitypath.com/enneagram/9-personality-types/

Type Eight: The Asserter. (n.d.). Leadership Greater Hartford. Retrieved May 17, 2023, from https://leadershipgh.org/enneagramprofiler/type-eight-the-asserter/

Type Eight: The Challenger. (n.d.). Enneagram Today. Retrieved May 17, 2023, from https://enneagramtoday.com/what-is-the-enneagram/type-8/

Type Five. (n.d.). The Enneagram Institute. https://www.enneagraminstitute.com/type-5

Type One. (n.d.). The Enneagram Institute. https://www.enneagraminstitute.com/type-1

Type Six: The Loyalist. (n.d.). Enneagram Academy. https://enneagramacademy.com/enneagram-types/type-six-the-loyalist

Type Two. (n.d.). The Enneagram Institute. https://www.enneagraminstitute.com/type-2

Vidal, M. A., & Gómez, J. (2016). Improving teamwork through the Enneagram. *Team Performance Management, 22*(1/2), 38–53. https://doi.org/10.1108/TPM-09-2014-0040

Wagner, J. (1980). A descriptive, reliability, and validity study of the Enneagram personality typology. *Dissertations.* https://ecommons.luc.edu/luc_diss/2109

Wagner, J. (2010, December 30). *History of the Enneagram.* The Enneagram Spectrum of Personality Styles. http://enneagramspectrum.com/173/history-of-the-enneagram/

Yuan, L. (2019, September 10). *Here's how you communicate, based on your Enneagram type.* Psychology Junkie. https://www.psychologyjunkie.com/heres-how-you-communicate-based-on-your-enneagram-type/